MUD SPACE & SPIRIT

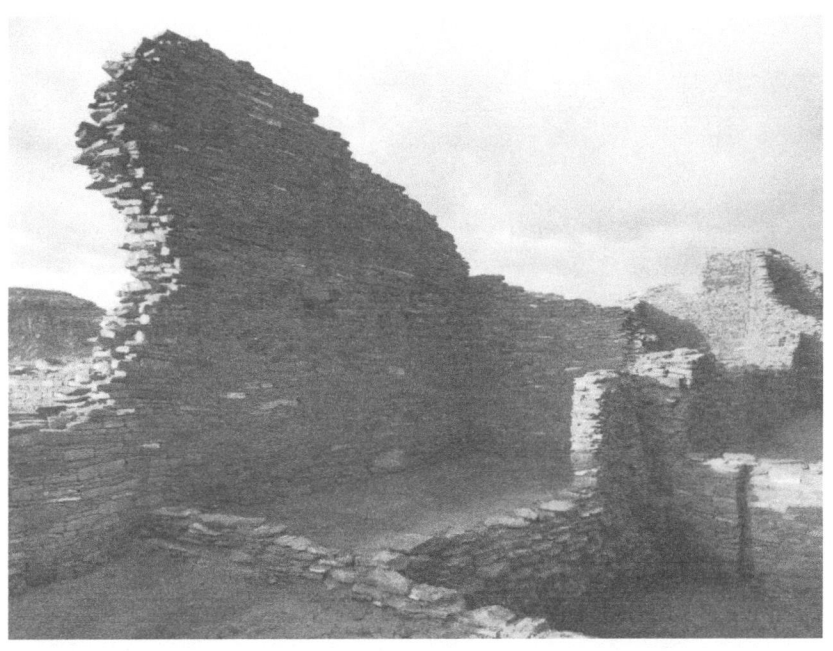

"The real history of the United States began, not on the narrow strip of Atlantic seaboard, but in the great Southwest. Long before the Pilgrim Fathers had been born, swarthy Spaniards were colonizing what is now the United States."

—CHARLES F. LUMMIS

MUD SPACE & SPIRIT
handmade adobes

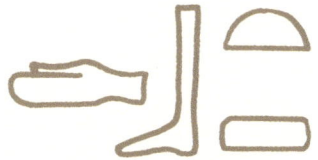

Text: Virginia Gray and Alan Macrae
Photography: Wayne McCall

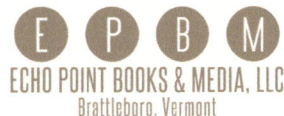

Published by Echo Point Books & Media
Brattleboro, Vermont
www.EchoPointBooks.com

All rights reserved.
Neither this work nor any portions thereof may be reproduced, stored in a retrieval system, or transmitted in any capacity without written permission from the publisher.

Copyright © 2022 by Alan Macrae & Wayne McCall

Mud, Space and Spirit
ISBN: 978-1-64837-106-6 (casebound)
       978-1-64837-107-3 (paperback)

Cover design by Kaitlyn Whitaker

Cover image: *Tower House* by Wayne McCall

FOREWORD

THESE HOUSES and the people who inhabit them are scattered through 5000 square miles of solitude in the Southwest's high desert. Most of them don't know each other and are meeting for the first time in his book. I see them together as a vanguard consciousness, loners in the middle of nowhere, at the end of a jeep road, or dug into a hill. Only the sun can find them. Their houses are self-portraits, ranging from rudimentary to sophisticated. Any resemblances come more from the prevailing powers of mud, space and spirit than from an exchange of personal inspiration.

Their environment is severe. Indians once called this Land of the Dancing Sun. Banshee winds sweep down from the Sangre de Cristo Mountains bringing snow to the desert floor. Yet the sun is dominant most of the year, converting mud into ceramic material. Earth, fire water — and space. The primal space of this high land makes people and all living things seem antlike, mere specks on the curvature of the horizon. Yet with hands and humble mud a human being can wall in personal space and bring himself back to life-size. Adobe is the natural flesh of walls out here, with the plasticity to be shaped in any way the builder conceives. Hands shovel mud into forms, turn bricks in the drying sun, lay them in walls; hands finally, in sweeping caresses, apply mud plaster, softening corners and blending masses. No house could be more handmade.

Mud is free, although the work can be rather formidable for a lone builder. People in this region sometimes rely on a phenomenon called strangers. "They came from nowhere," a builder told me, "and the walls seemed to rise up out of the earth. Then when it was done, the strangers disappeared and I found myself alone with my house." He was describing the spirit of being solitary, yet unalone.

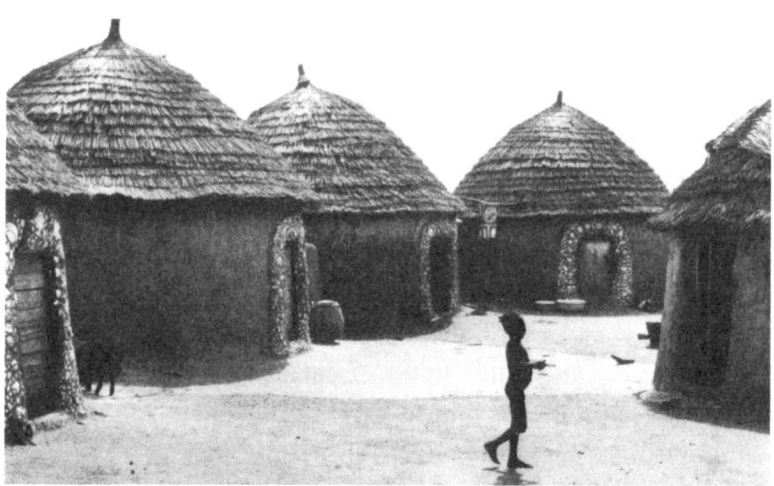

I spent some time in the foothills late last winter when the red willows, dark elms and silvery cottonwoods were getting ready for spring. I slept high in the Tree Room where I could see mountain snow and feel the warm hug of adobe walls. Piñon smoke from four or five fireplaces sweetened the air. I could have been in Africa, or Arabia, Spain, a Pueblo *kiva*, or a territorial fort. I could have been back 7000 years in Mesopotamia, a Neolithic farmer, running my hand over the mud-plastered wall, feeling the course of original hands. This has always been. No tool is more sensitive than the fingers, no implement better adapted than the hand. Clay yields to pressure in building as it does in pottery. Some of the houses I saw were giant pots with fireplaces resembling urns and high vases.

We are said to have risen from the primeval ooze, told that the cradle of civilization lies on the Dark Continent. I chanced upon some photographs of mud villages in Sudan, houses shaped like bee hives and loaves of bread, women rubbing the walls. The houses are close, even touching with common walls—human termitaries. This is a mud commune in tribal Africa, walls livened by stripes of oxides or herringbone textures pressed from ears of corn. The reedy roofs are stalks of millet after the grain has been winnowed.

I am in a mud room in Santa Fe, mind you, studying the compact geometry of African villages, when suddenly my mind leaps to the Arizona desert where Soleri is building a city of tomorrow, to contain 30,000 people, yet occupying no more earth space than a large villa. Tomorrow's vision; yesterday's being ghostly cliff dwellings, hived pueblos, clustered Mediterranean villages and Spanish colonial towns.

I wondered if these communal visions had any bearing, or could give any enlightenment upon these widely separated and

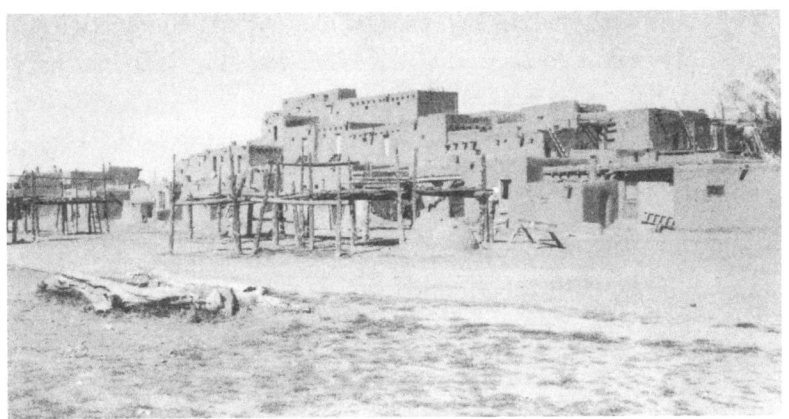

unique adobe houses I visited. Here in the austere desert where the architecture is mud and the clock is slow, I am seeing personal histories—not tribal, environmental, or historic. Though each builder came by his own road, for his own reasons, I began hearing words in their language referring to a common consciousness. The first word was hope. Then came sun and wind. The technological-minded among them used the terms heliostats, tracking lenses, sun pillows, energy retrieval systems and thermal flywheels. Words from the 21st century. Yet today, with a deliberate consciousness I have not been aware of in the past, they concentrate on their southern walls. Many houses face south to use the sun for growing and heating. Their ingenuity would be hard to surpass. At the same time, with windows, they keep watch on the northern peaks and the dawns and sunsets of the desert land, all the while enclosed in the harbor of earthen walls.

These people adapt and yield to nature in ways most of us have forgotten, if we ever knew. Their relationship with House is symbiotic. Adobe serves as long as it is lived in. Abandoned, it will slowly settle back into earth. Each year the winter's wash from weathering walls must be scooped up and used to heal them. Man and earth, keeping each other alive.

The techniques of adobe building are well documented in other books. This one was first conceived as a simple portrayal of individual imaginations working with mud; a fantasy book for readers locked in urban life, or an encouragement to freer spirits. Now the book is assembled, more needs to be asked. There is the question of personal space and expression, both the poetics and realities of space. San Francisco poet, Lawrence Fixel, said, "Your space to swing your arms ends where my nose begins." Ideas of freedom are aroused. Solitary heart and social animal. The cliff dwellings may have been tribal hives, while Soleri's cities suggest a double helix of anonymous bunk beds. The condominium to end them all.

The houses in this book are bursts of spirit, each unique from the other and far away, yet made from common materials on common Southwestern land. The diversity of walls, for example. While consensus favors curving space, some find security in square corners and "masculine" angles. Such an array of phobias and manias—nest rooms versus castles, planning against improvisation, symmetry opposed to free form, ruggedness compared to finesse, claustrophobia and vertigo. Two houses are completely underground, no silhouette to disturb the horizon. Another is perched on a high mountain ridge, where an eagle would be. Yet all of them are built from mud, the trunks of ponderosa pines, peeled aspen saplings, and split cedar.

These new age pioneers taught me a new word—growhole. The southern walls of many of their houses open into a growhole, a greenhouse or solarium, dug below floor level, where vegetables and flowers flourish through the year. You find zucchini, cucumber, tomato, and chili ripening when snow lies outside. You can feel gentle heat rise from growhole into the house, soft humidity spreading through the arid air, fresh with oxygen. The "chimney" effect of the growhole functions well in this severe land. As far as we know this is new, the passive use of the sun upon adobe buildings conceived much like their ancestors 7000 years ago.

While elsewhere more people are going back to the land, these visionary troglodytes are literally going *into* the land, burrowing in and pulling earthen walls like cloaks over their shoulders. I wondered if they were hiding from the world, if they blinked in the light of day. As I walked through their cave rooms and grottos, my shadow was on the floor. The conventional window looks across the land, but here were not only skylights, but entire roofs of light. Light pours down and floods the rooms. The awareness of sky and uses of the sun! Plants to cultivate, eat, and smell thrive in their rooms and growholes. I'm impressed how much at home these people are with the primal elements of nature. I don't call that hiding.

I'm awed by their imagination too, and what their hands have done. I look down at my clean fingernails and wish for mud.

—NOEL YOUNG

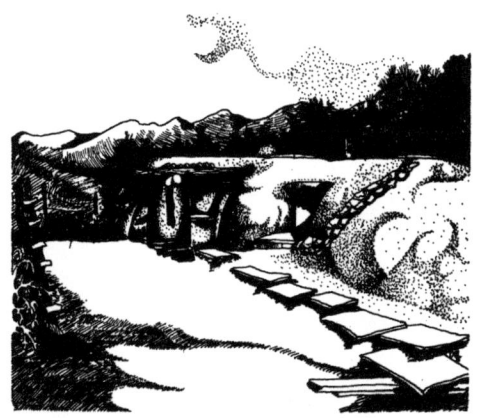

THE VANISHING ENJARRADORA

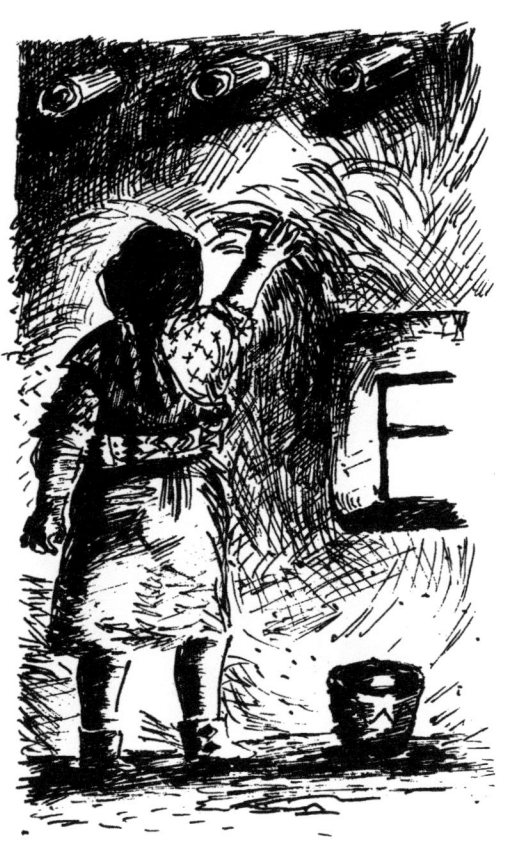

TRADITIONAL Spanish architecture is fading from the Southwest, slowly melting back into the earth from which it grew. Adobe construction techniques and practices, refined by four hundred years of continuous use and recorded only in the oral tradition of the people, are disappearing too. The presence of the woman builder, the *enjarradora,* is very old in the Southwest, rooted deep in the Chicana's Indian past.

The Spanish, soon after their conquest of the Southwest and the building of the great missions, adopted the custom of the *enjarradora*. Indian men easily adopted Spanish innovations in carpentry, for woodworking was already a familiar skill. But Indian women were the undisputed experts in earthen construction. Of course, under the circumstances of communal labor, everyone did everything at one time or another, but mud working was virtually unthinkable for Indian men. Generally, men played a supportive role as *suqueteros*, or mud mixers. They built scaffolds and supplied the women with *suquete* and water, as they do today among the Indians and the Raza.

Certain processes and stages of adobe work have become associated exclusively with women. To the *enjarradora,* broadly "plasteress" in English, belong the final phases of construction, the finishing. The *enjarradora* gives the whole architecture its final shape, color and detail.

A long isolation (and one so rudely broken) has given native culture in the Southwest an individuality naturally expressed in its architecture. Adobe building, once universal, has almost ceased. Ironically, the people who can least afford it are the Raza, the people who know it best. The pace of modern life is hostile to the more contemplative skills. Amid the hustle of the "modern construction trade," there is no place for adobe handwork and through disuse the long transmission of techniques nears an end.

With the disappearance of adobe building we lose not only ancient processes, but a whole ambience that enrichens the very texture of our lives. Take *alisando*, a process fallen into almost total disuse. *Alisando* is the last step in adobe building, a mud painting both decorative and functional. There are many places in the desert where the earth has a particularly beautiful color and where the *enjarradora* goes for her materials. Some of these sites, through generations of excavation, have become pits sunk fifty feet into the earth. Others are secret places, known only to discreet individuals whose use of colored earth has religious connations.

Once the clay has been carried to the building site, it is processed—soaked, settled, skimmed and treated according to its particular characteristics. The *alisa*, or mud, is mixed with *polidas* and applied as a final finish to adobe walls, using sheepskin rather than a brush. This gives the wall a suede-like texture and luminosity often enhanced by the addition of mica. Although as smooth as human skin, the walls are not mechanically flat and evoke the sense of living earth—"Madre Tierra" to the *enjarradora*. *Alisando* produces colorful highlights to grace the mouths of fireplaces, arches, and niches. The lower section of a portal wall might be finished in, say, *tierra amarilla*—a pale ochre reflecting light from an infinity of mica particles.

Alisando works a thin layer of fine clay into the surface, sealing it. Though not waterproof, water tends to roll off without gathering abrasive particles—erosion is reduced and less moisture penetrates. Annual replastering is a quick and easy

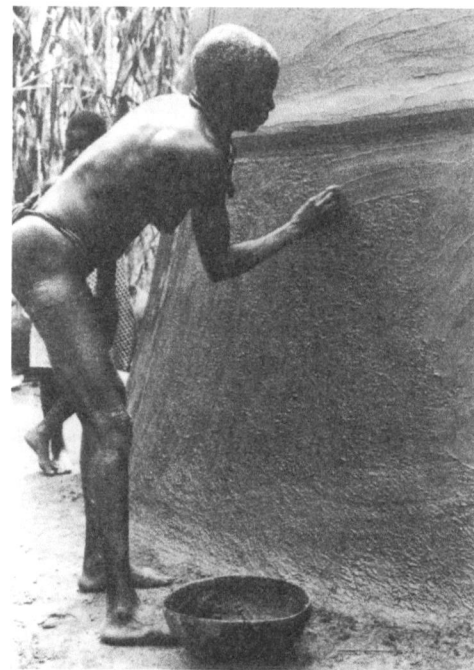

It began in Africa.

chore and the materials may be stored for years as it was by women who also built the fireplaces, maintained the village church and did all the repairs that kept adobe walls standing for centuries.

Recently, cement plaster has been used to protect adobe from rain. Cement not only fails its practical purpose, but has created a great esthetic loss and put the *enjarradora* out of work. Cement and earth are incompatible; they expand and contract at different rates. The inside of cement plaster sweats. Adobe not only expands and contracts—it settles. Rigid cement cannot respond to the movement of adobe and eventually the cement must crack. Water seeps in, freezing, thawing and deteriorating the walls. All this happens behind an innocent-looking exterior until the day of reckoning.

The story of the *enjarradora* is still audible in Spanish oral history and legible in the walls that bear her handprints. Construction, in those days, was part of a collective lifestyle. It is illuminating to find women playing so vital and visible a role in literally housing God and Man. Though we cannot know what degree of esthetic leadership the *enjarradora* actually wielded on the construction site without a deeper discussion of her cultural role, we can assume that those *enjarradoras* did not climb scaffolds to execute someone else's esthetic judgments. No, passing final judgment on the plaster the *suqueteros* mixed, the *enjarradora* took the living flesh of the earth in hand and fused the roles of architect and laborer.

—ANITA RODRIGUEZ

(*The spirit of the* enjarradora *revived is evident on the following pages, beginning with Sally Edelman, who shaped a mural dragon from colored earths, as well as Rachel Brown, Loreen Pearson and Virginia Gray herself. The men, you will see, have turned much of their attention to growholes, greenhouses, and solar technology.*)

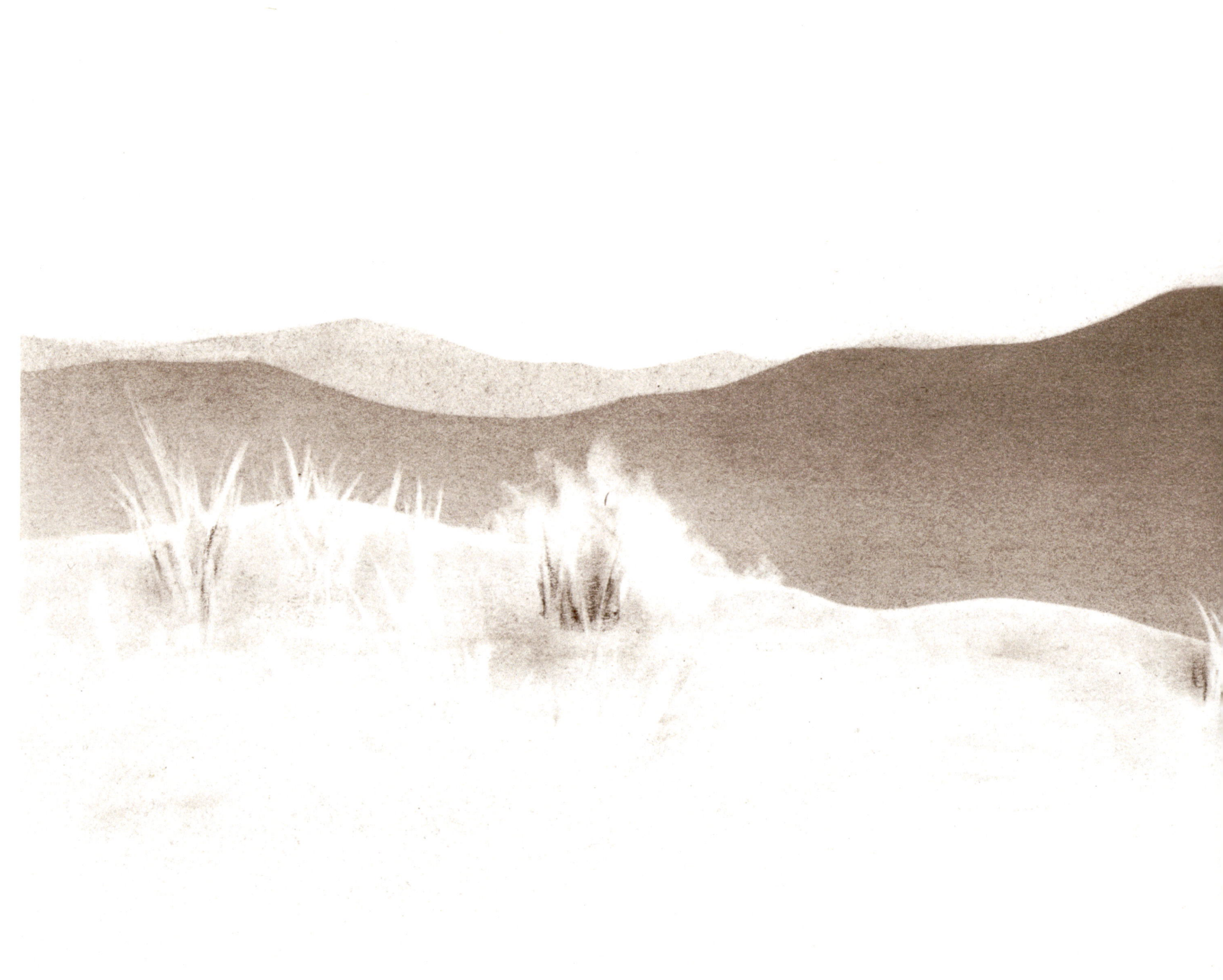

DRAGON HOUSE

SALLY EDELMAN's house is near the mountains, 8200 feet high and there's heavy snow in the winter. She began building in 1970 and the house has evolved differently from her original ideas. She studied painting in art school, but working with mud was her first experience in sculpture.

SALLY: I planned just a peaked roof house and I'd seen a picture of a Mexican house with a porch somewhat like this one. I had a commune put up the walls, though they didn't finish it because I ran out of money. There were about ten people working on the house at one point because I didn't have power up here then; no cement mixer for the mud or the adobes, and all the latillas had to be cut by hand. It took maybe four months just to get the walls up, but we all had a really good time—drank a lot of beer—and it was fun.

Once the walls were up, instead of a peaked roof, I decided I wanted something more far out. I thought of putting up a geodesic dome, but when I saw they were made of plywood I said no to that. So I designed the domed ceiling with matchsticks. That part got built really quickly—my nephew made the skylight and I did the stained glass. A friend carved the pillars with a chain saw.

The first winter I spent here the roof wasn't even finished. We had the latillas up and then blankets and plastic on top. The floor was still dirt and whenever a kid walked through there were billows of dust . . . it was a hard

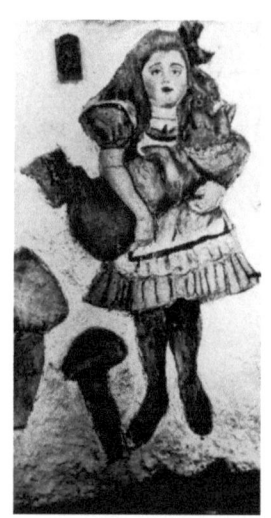

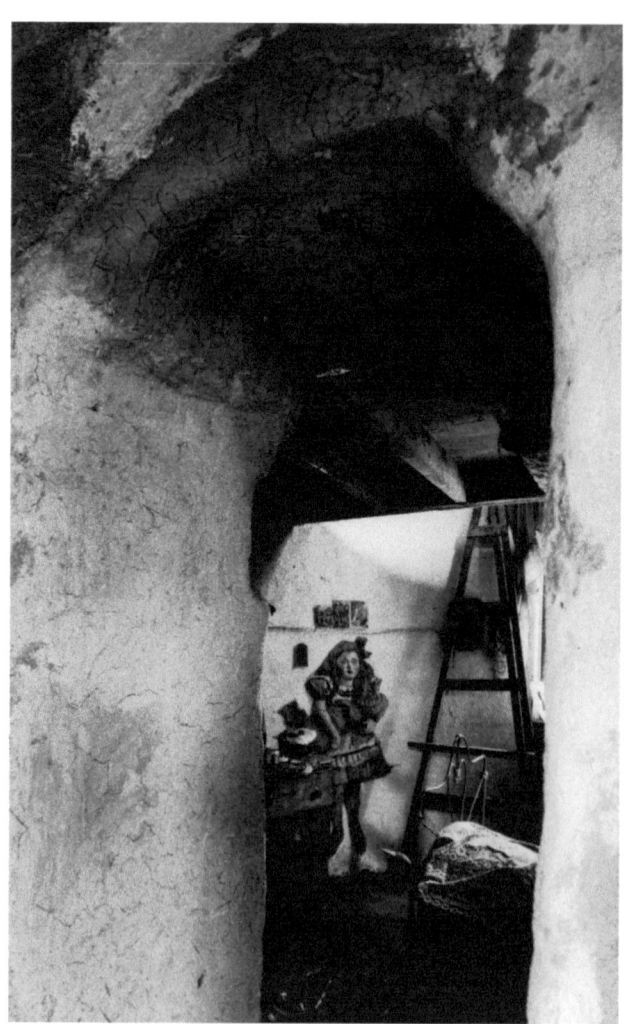

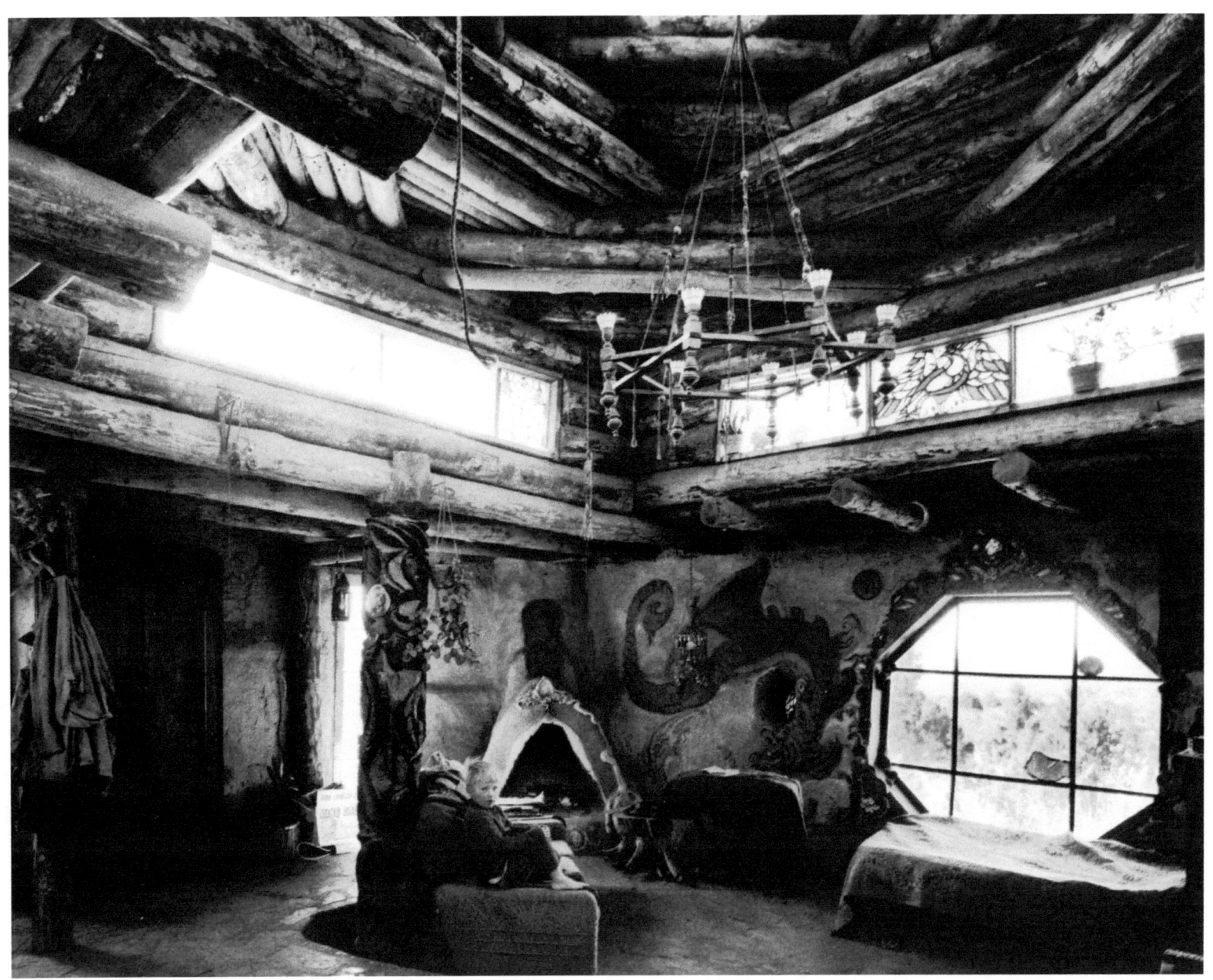

winter. Then my husband finished the roof. Living is easier now—we've got electricity in, and the road is ploughed in winter.

We've decided to put a loft in because even with a really good wood stove, an Ashley, it's hard to heat along in December. I love the space because it feels real open to me, so we're going to put vigas up with boards on top which can be taken down in the summer.

I started mudding the outside of the house and thought—I'd much rather be piddling with the mud instead. The first piece I tried fell off the wall, so I put nails in about every six inches. I had to do it several times until I got what I wanted. The dragon was easier—I just did it, mostly in a day. Then I went around, all over the place, getting different colors of earth to use as slip coatings. Now I have to get some blue dirt; that'll be my next find.

The tower wasn't part of my peaked roof house idea. Originally I was going to build a very simple house, then as I got to thinking about it I realized how flexible adobe really is. As a kid I wanted to live in a castle, to be a fairy, and in my fantasies I always wanted a house like this. It's slow, maybe it won't be really finished for another five years, but that doesn't bother me.

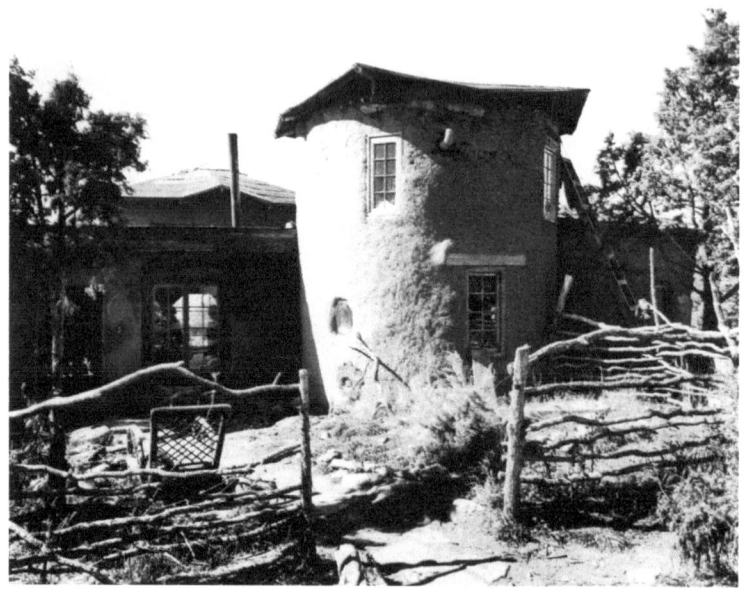

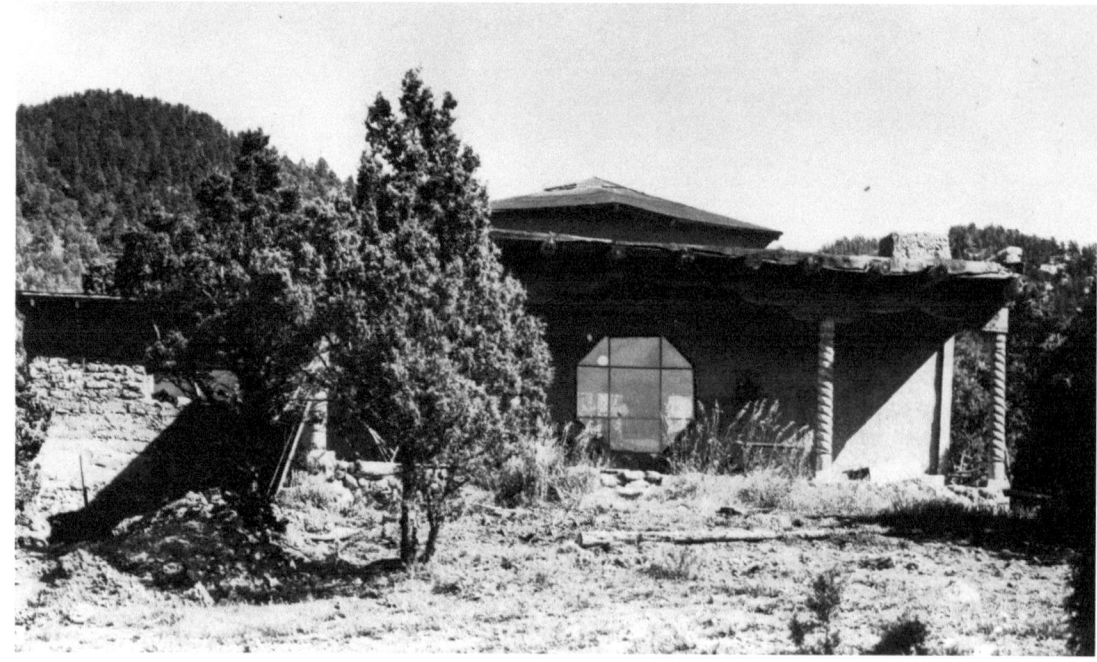

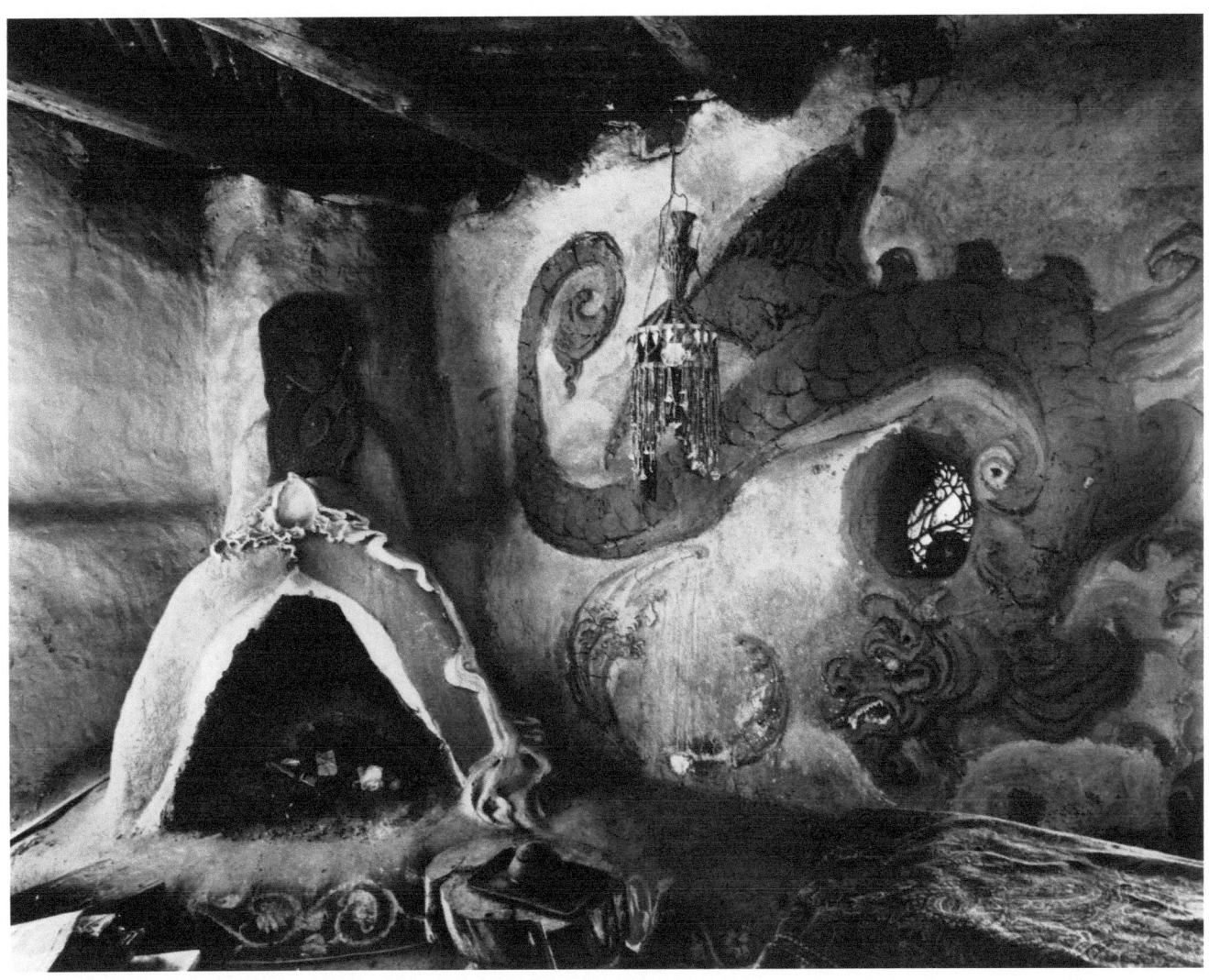

SEVEN LEVELS

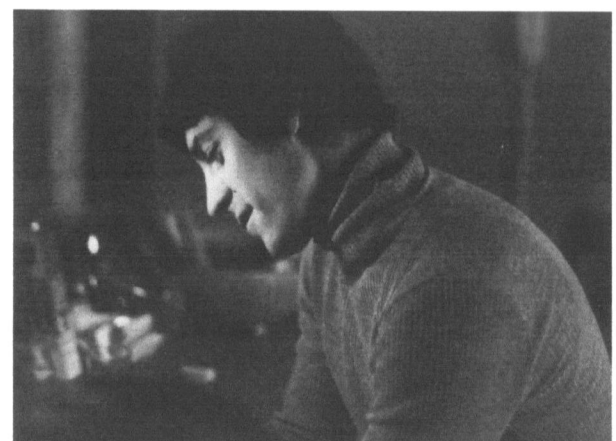

ED *and* VICKI SANDOVAL *built their house in a long-settled community that is still partly agricultural. Ed is a high school art teacher, makes jewelry, paints, and works with wood. Vicki is a nurse. They have two children. Their house is on seven levels, with some rooms partially underground.*

ED: I love entering a house with different levels. It's always intrigued me.

VICKI: In Utah we lived in a sub-division and it drove me crazy. I wanted a house with breaks here and there so it wouldn't be monotonous.

ED: The only way to have what you want is to build it yourself. We spent two years on the plans. I'd had some architectural classes in school, but nothing advanced. I made blueprints and renderings, so I knew pretty well what was going to develop. When you look at a floorplan you imagine walls going up,

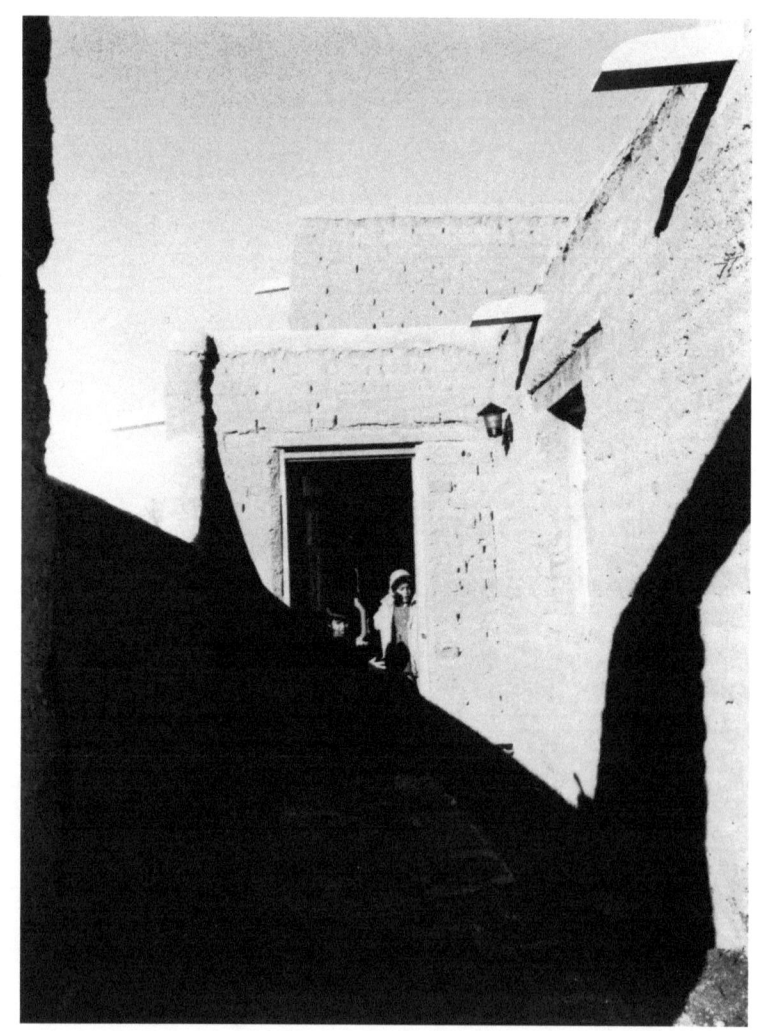

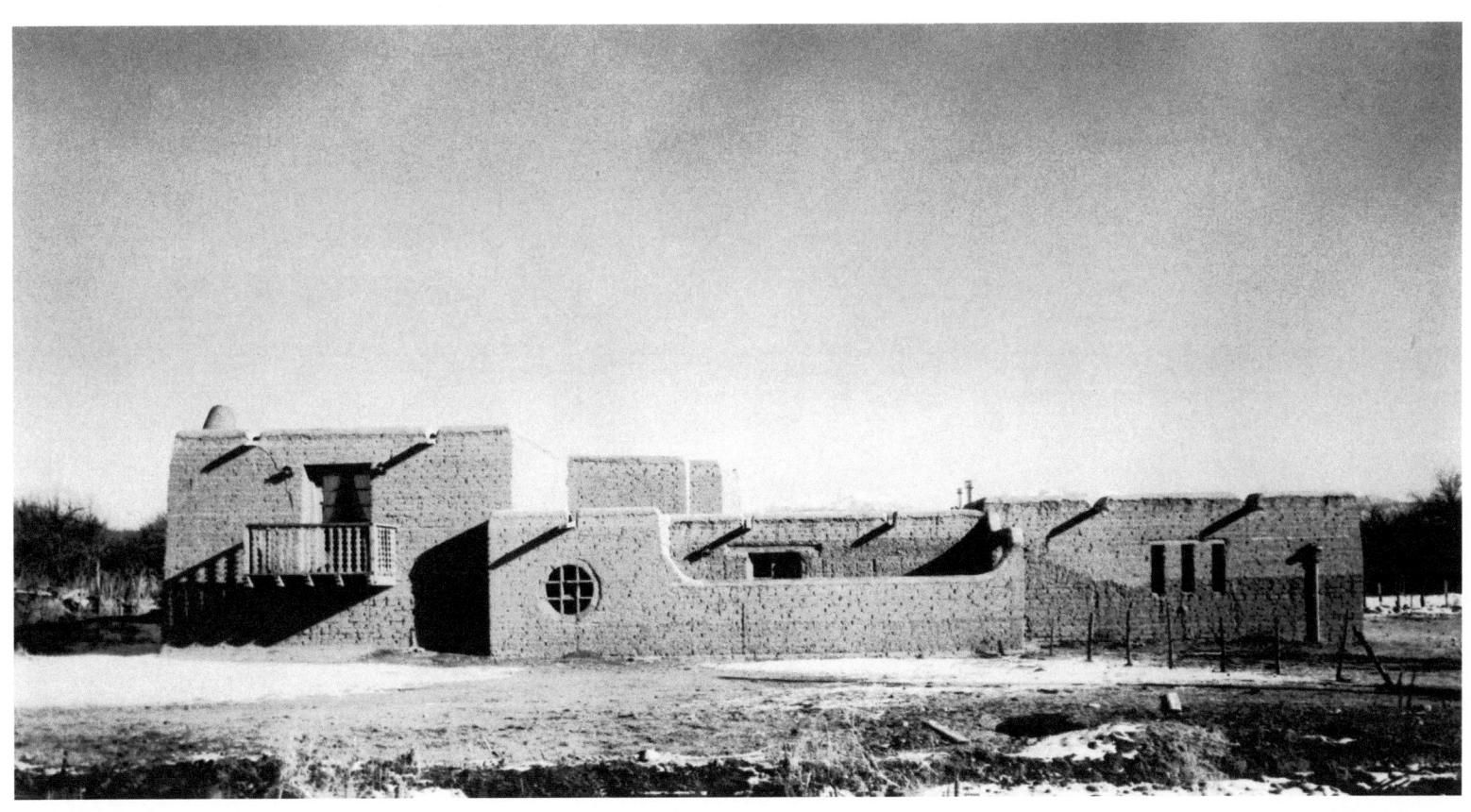

but sometimes you don't realize they might project higher than you visualized and develop surprising breaks and designs.

The Sandoval's use of materials and building techniques is traditional in northern New Mexico.

ED: All the adobes were made right here from the excavation dirt. In the spring we had almost every inch of this property covered with bricks—you could hardly move around. Off and on all summer we made adobes to keep up with the building. We've used 23,000 so far and we're still going.

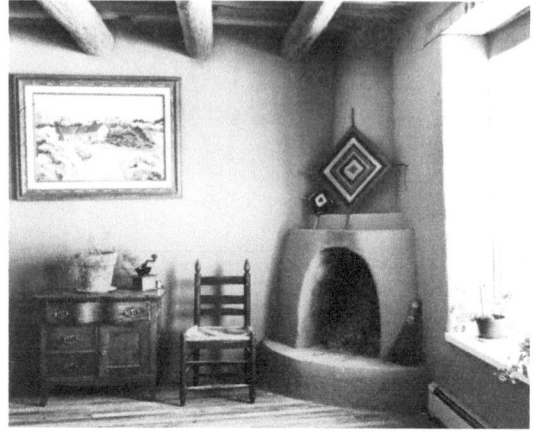

Some of the vigas are from an old house; they're a hundred years old and hand-squared. Most of them came from a canyon in the mountains. We got a pair of mules to drag logs out of the forest to be loaded on a truck. We had fun getting them, but that first day I thought I'd never get the house built. Then the next day it snowed eighteen inches. We found a deserted cabin where we spent the night. A good thing the mules were along or we might never have gotten out.

I had the summer free to work on the house and hired some people to help. A fellow teacher did the plumbing. A neighbor who was just going to show us how to build fireplaces, got so enthused he went from room to room making the fireplaces himself. He built them in the old way and they work beautifully.

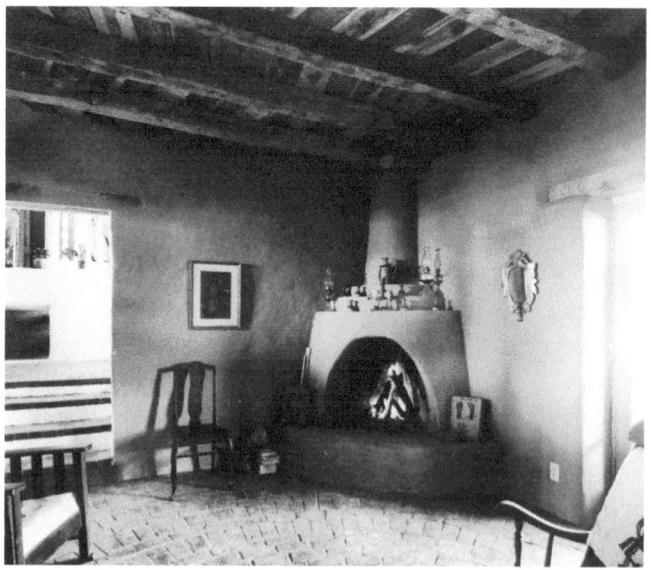

The exterior walls are traditional—two adobes thick.

ED: A lot of people came by with advice. The old-timers couldn't believe the double walls. They were kids when they last saw walls built this way.

VICKI: I think we brought back a lot of memories to the old people around here. They'd stop by every few days and often remembered something they felt we should know.

ED: You meet many beautiful people whether you take their advice or not.

The house was begun in Spring 1974. Ed and Vicki moved in a year and a half later.

ED: My mom said it was a miracle it went up so fast.

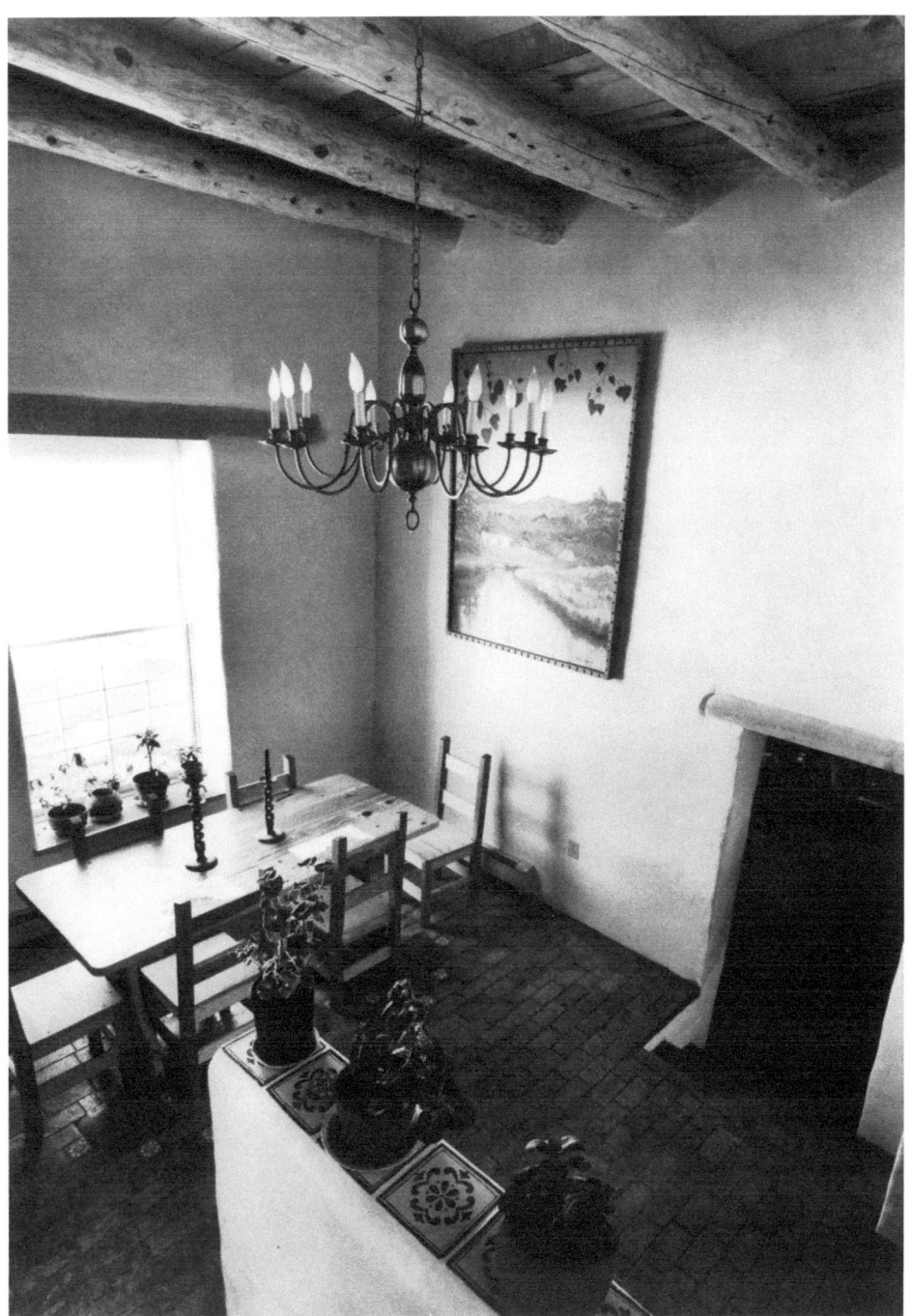

UNICORN HOUSE

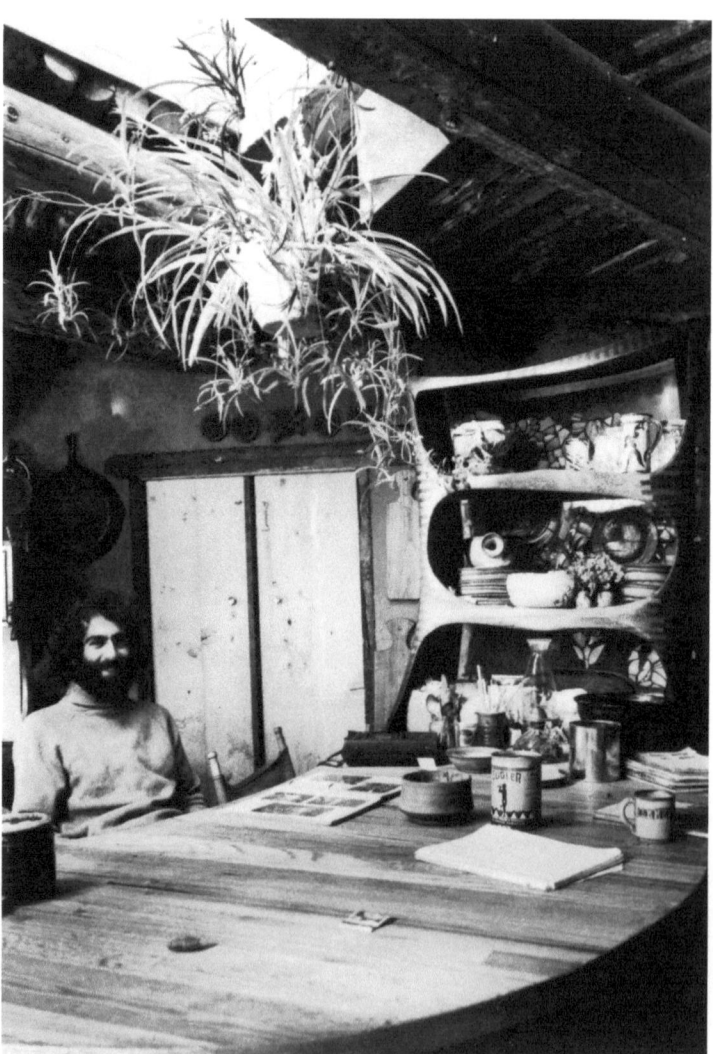

TED ULLMAN had never been an artist. He couldn't draw, never attended art classes and planned to be a businessman when he grew up. Then came the Vietnam war.

TED: I was going to be a pilot until I realized I didn't want to drop bombs on Vietnam. I figured I'd better do things that were a little more constructive than the business world or the military.

Then came the mountains . . . it started in Colorado where I first wanted to build a house. I didn't find a place I really liked so I just kept wandering until spring. Then I said to myself "Hey, let's build a house in the country," which seemed like a neat thing to do. I spent a year looking before I found this land.

Ted's plan was very simple. He drew three shapes: a big oval in the center, a rectangle for a greenhouse to the south and a round tower to the north.

A friend who's an incredible sketch artist came by while I was building and he would draw what I was talking about. I'd look at his sketches and wonder if it was going to come out the same. It came out pretty close.

Then another friend suggested I make a wall between the oval and the tower and put in a pantry. I'm really thankful because without the pantry I would've been in a real mess. The kitchen is too small as it is, but I wasn't much into kitchens then since I'd

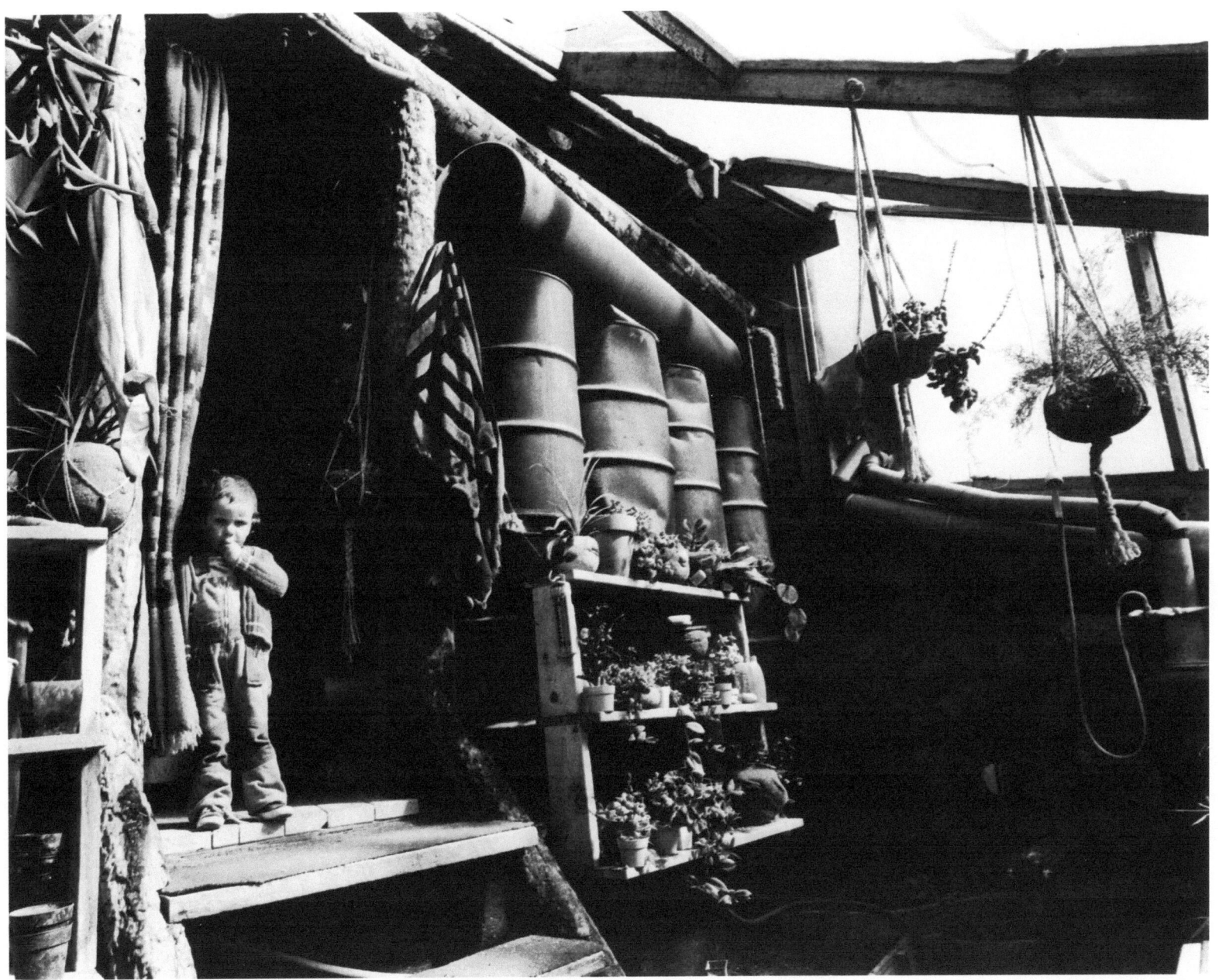

always been living in small apartments and eating in Chinese restaurants.

In Ted's greenhouse, near the kitchen, he grows vegetables all year long. The greenhouse also heats the house since the dividing wall is stacked with black metal drums filled with water. They collect heat during the day and radiate warmth at night.

I got the idea for the greenhouse and barrels from Steve Baer. I also found Ken Kern's book, *The Owner-Built Home,* immensely useful; figuring out what you want, what a house is to be and how you hope to live in it. I wanted to have views, but not big panoramas because they would lure me outdoors. I want to feel comfortable when I'm doing things indoors, but I don't want to feel like I'm outside when I'm inside. I like a real contrast.

Ted began building in April 1974. He gardened and played some music but spent most of his time working on the house.

For the work it takes to build a comfortable house—finished to the point where you can sit for five days and the wind doesn't blow through—it's such a pleasure to live in. Even if the chimney does smoke, it's an incredible feeling doing your own house rather than buying one. What I learned was amazing. In two years I learned about tools, about art, about forms and architecture. I learned to mix cement, to dig footings, to lay adobes,

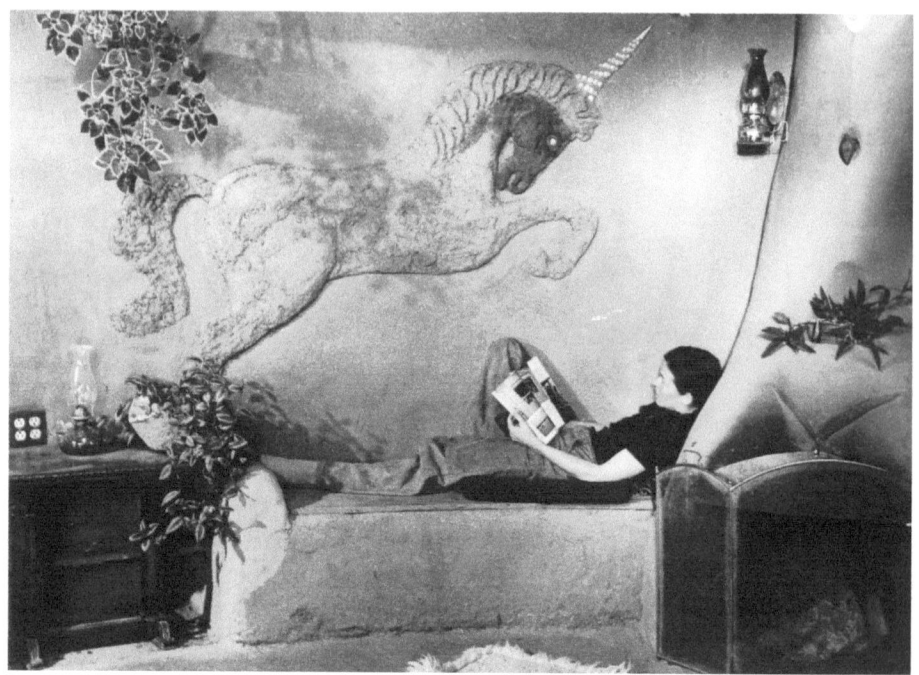

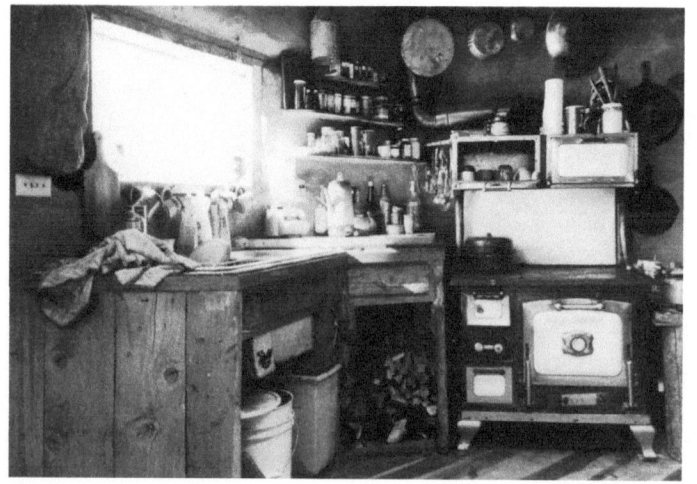

to use line levels and how to plaster. When I finish the bedroom I feel confident I'll be a fairly decent carpenter.

And then came the oval shape—it's been really comfortable to live in. Corners distract me. Here when I'm looking for something I can just spin around and find it. I built it big to avoid clutter. It's great to have enough space so you can bring in twenty or thirty people without feeling crowded. It's the impromptu dance hall for this area.

Ted attributes much to the influence of Gaudi and Bufano. After seeing Bufano's sculpture and mosaics in California he came back and began doing mosaics himself, and is getting involved with pottery and sculpture.

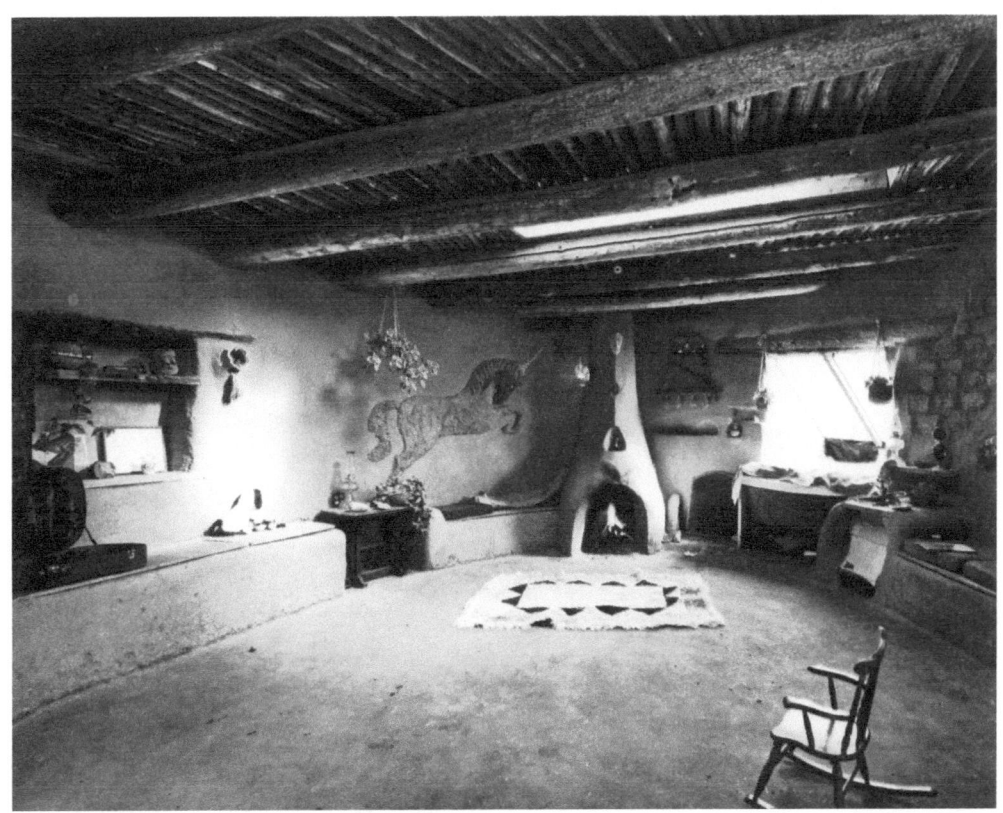

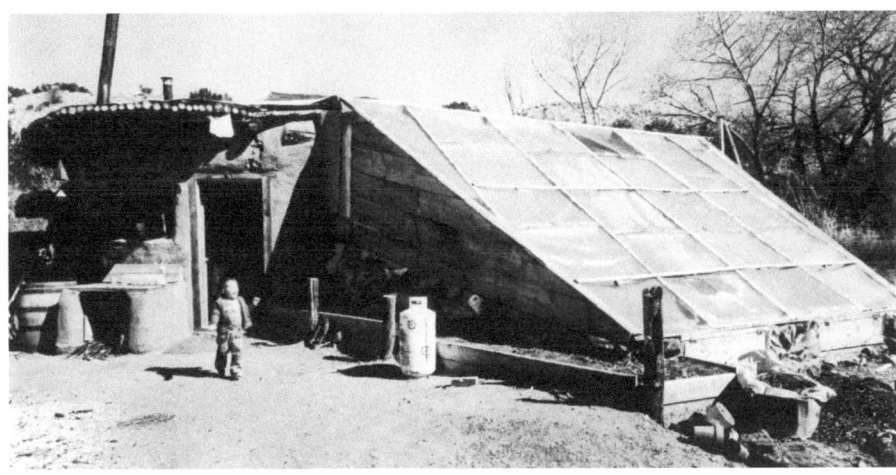

Ted's growhole.

Twenty years ago MALCOLM BROWN *and his family built a large, comfortable house using the ancient techniques of the Pueblo Indians. They built foundations of stone and mud mortar; the walls were puddled adobe, three feet thick at the base and tapering to a foot at the top. They mud-plastered the walls inside and out in the* enjarradora *tradition. The floors were poured mud mixed with straw, troweled smooth and sealed with oil and turpentine.*

The heart of the house is a spacious round living room and kitchen dominated by an enormous Ponderosa pole supporting the roof. A large window box with sloping glass brings in a roomful of morning light. Traditional building methods combined with a disciplined imagination created an exceptional house which has had a strong influence on other builders in the region. It is a powerful example of a family home.

A recent trip to India and the Far East reversed Malcolm's building ethic. After living on houseboats with a dozen others sharing the same cooking and recreational facilities, he now feels that private dwellings are a luxury of the past. Philosophically, his thoughts approach Paolo Soleri's. He sees the need for people to live communally in harmony with each other and the planet. This concept, he urgently feels, is the only way to protect the dwindling energy resources of the earth.

UMBRELLA ROOM

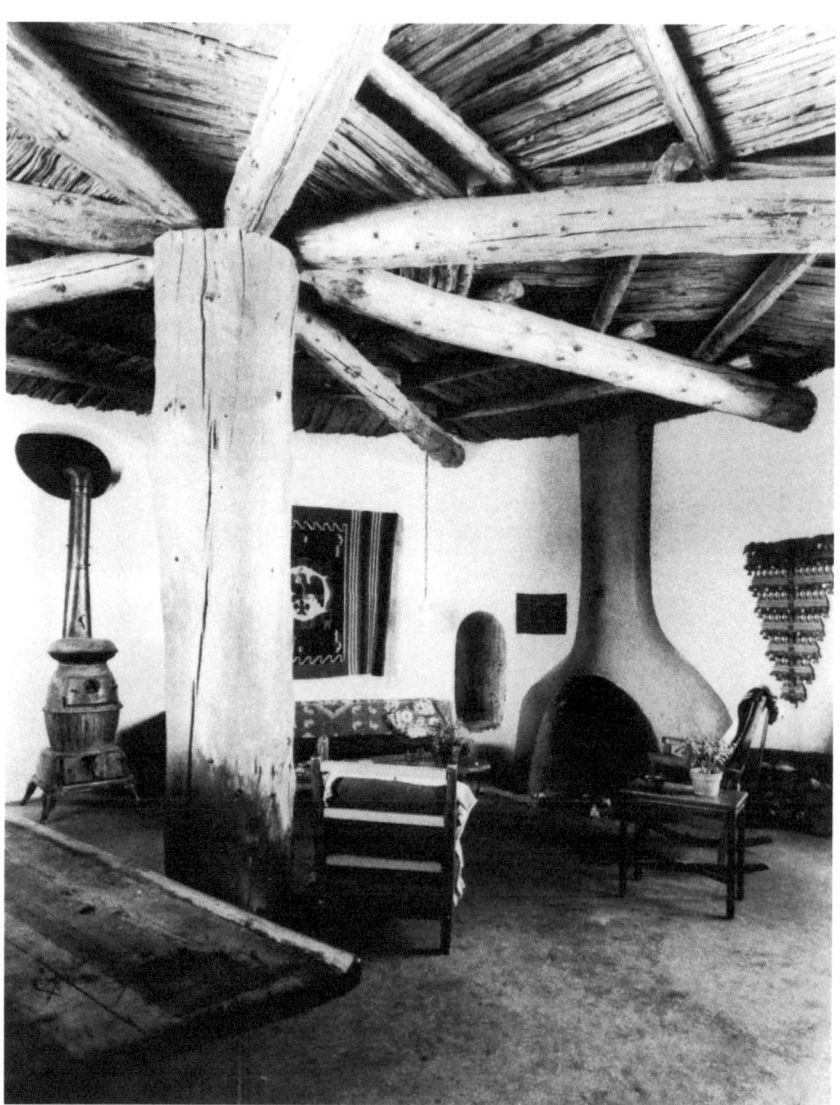

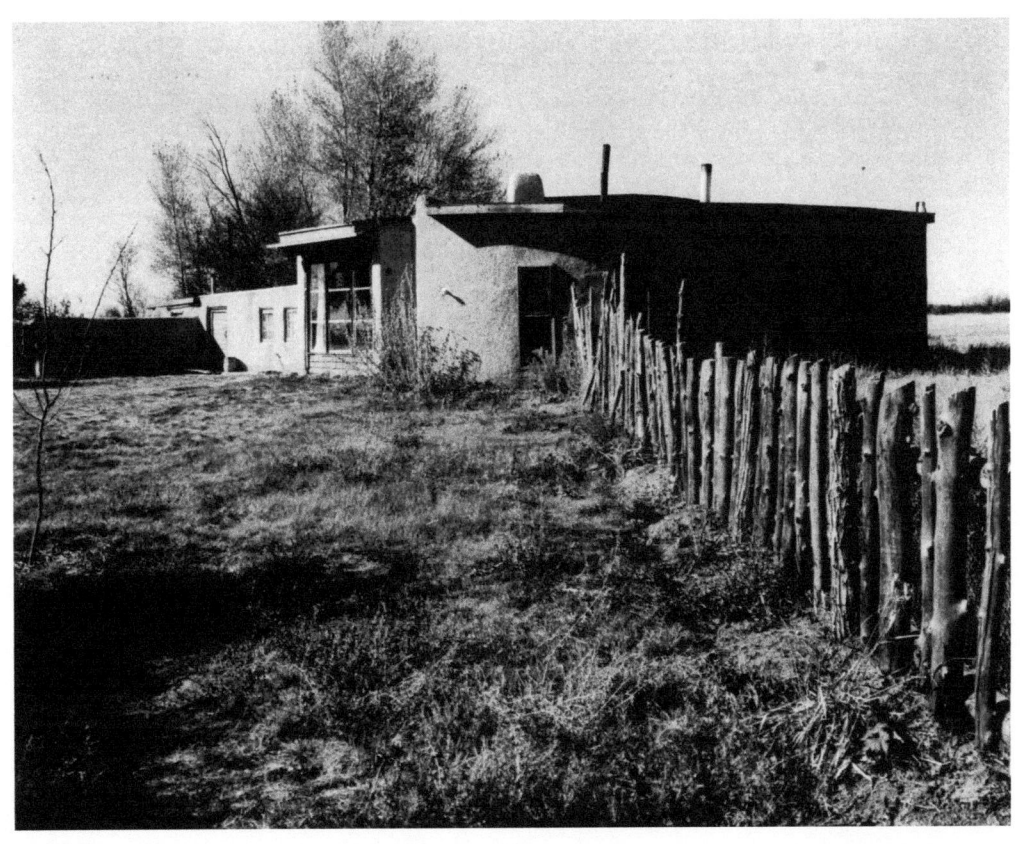

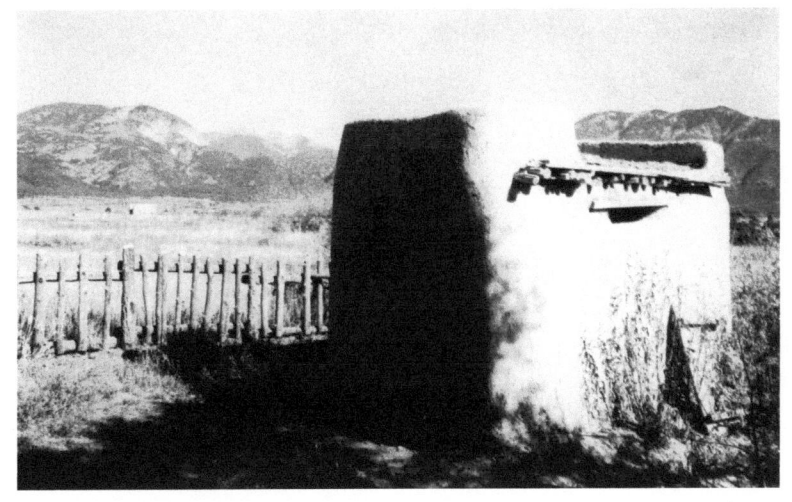

HARRY *and* LORENE PEARSON *call themselves "rocky mountaineers." They built their first house in Wyoming a number of years ago, according to Lorene's design. In 1945 they moved to New Mexico and built several more houses before they started their present compound in 1957. Harry is a retired agricultural economist and likes to weave.*

HARRY: Lorene's the architect. She is also a writer and a gourmet cook, so the house is almost all books and kitchen.

LORENE: Men think of houses from the outside, but women have to live in houses: the kitchen is a woman's idea. I love tools, particularly in the kitchen. Many people shut things away and don't like to see everything showing, but here it's all out in the open. Also, I don't like boxes or being closed in. I love to cook but I don't want to be in a cubbyhole; here I can cook and still be included in the conversation.

I like rooms to flow and don't like them square, so this house doesn't have many doors, though we can pull doors across our bedroom.

The houses the Pearsons built have not been changed by subsequent owners. Their building ideas suit many other people.

LORENE: I don't start designing until we have the lot. Then I try all kinds of things; placing the house on the site and organizing interior spaces to develop the general plan. I put storage space everywhere. Inside partitions are

30

A GROTTO

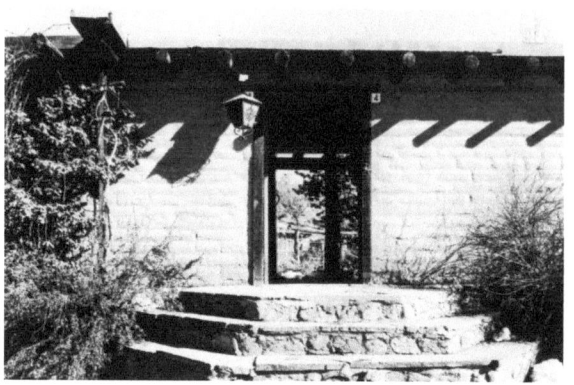

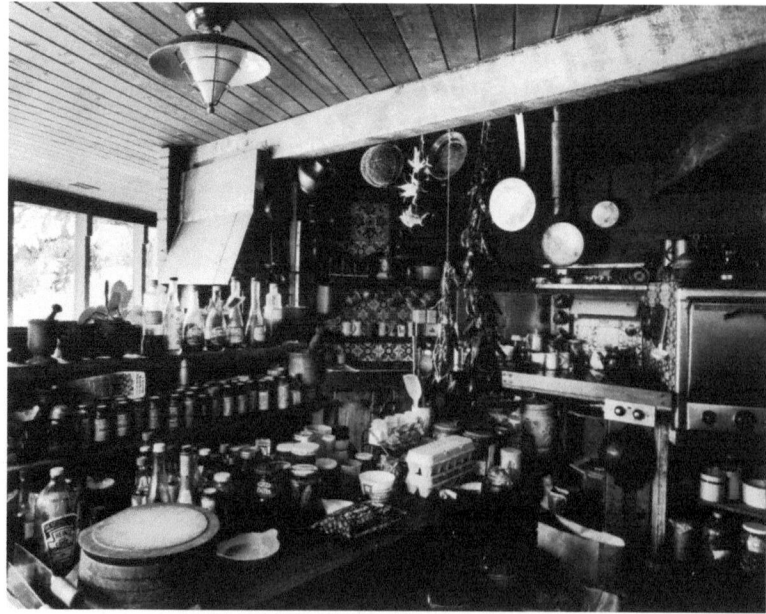

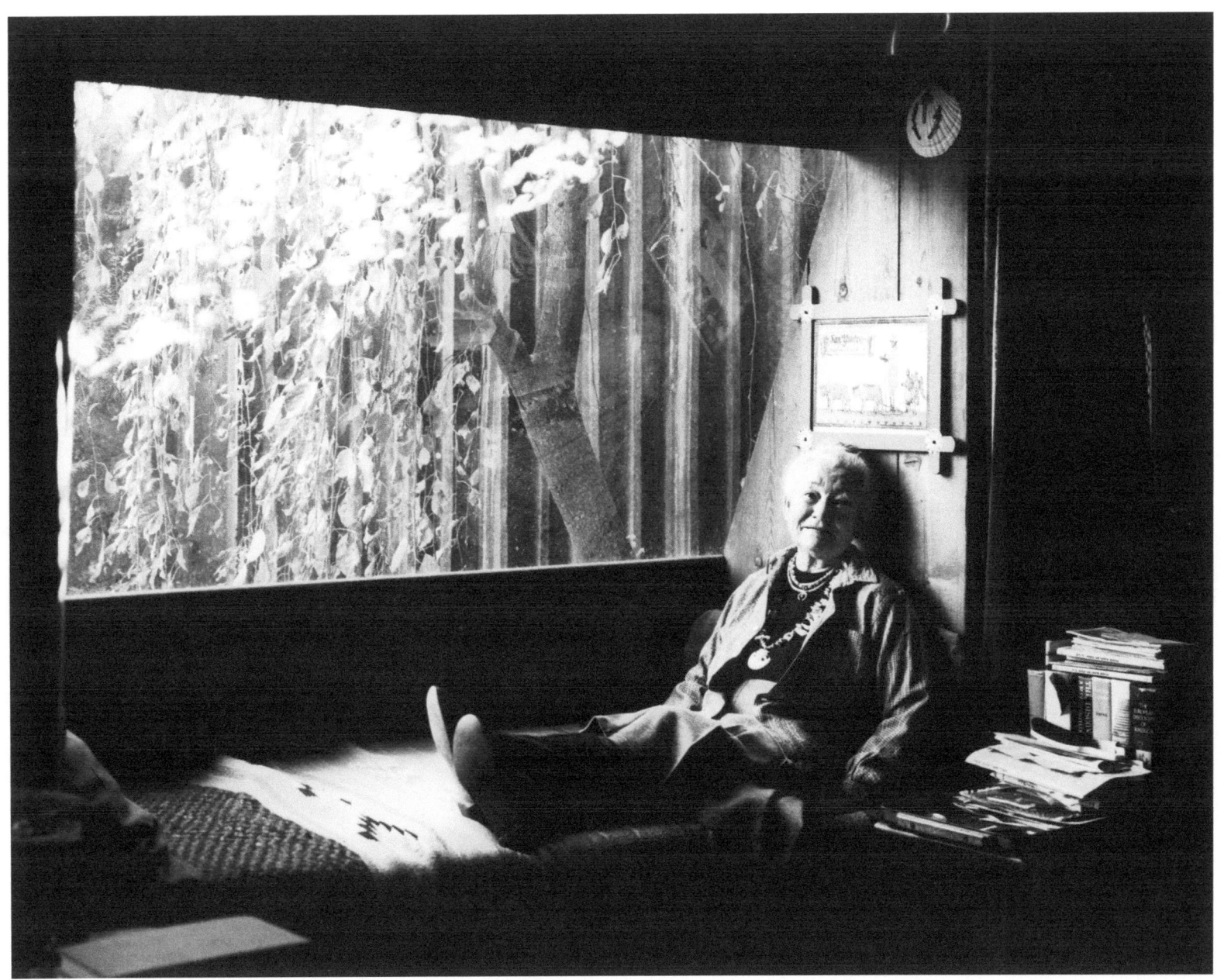

not simple walls, but cupboards and cabinets as well. I rarely have more than three weeks before construction begins so I really work hard. I don't believe you should start out and just add on and on. Doing it that way is a very hazardous business.

HARRY: In Caracas, where we lived for two years, houses are built right on the street. Then you pass through a *zaguan,* or little passageway, and it's all very private back there. We like that building tradition very much and used it here. We don't have windows on the street; that helps keep out dust. We draw fresh air from the patio.

The patio and garden are defined on one side by Harry's "loom room" and two apartments on the other side of the patio. Their house has a long southern exposure. In the winter the sunlight comes clear across the living room, bringing considerable warmth. In the summer an overhanging eave keeps out the sun. There is also Lorene's sewing room, filled with plants and an assortment of colorful material.

HARRY: Lorene's study is up in the rocks behind the house, like a grotto. We dug out the stone and used it to build with. It's self-contained and includes a small kitchen and a bathroom.

LORENE: Years ago we visited ancient Indian ruins that gave a feeling of being *in* the earth. My study is in the earth, very much like the cave where we all began. In a cave you are free from the outside world.

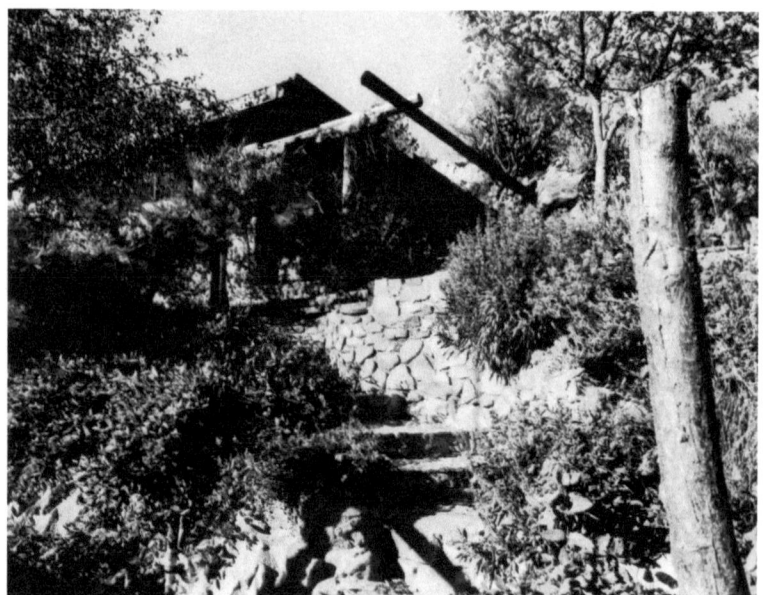

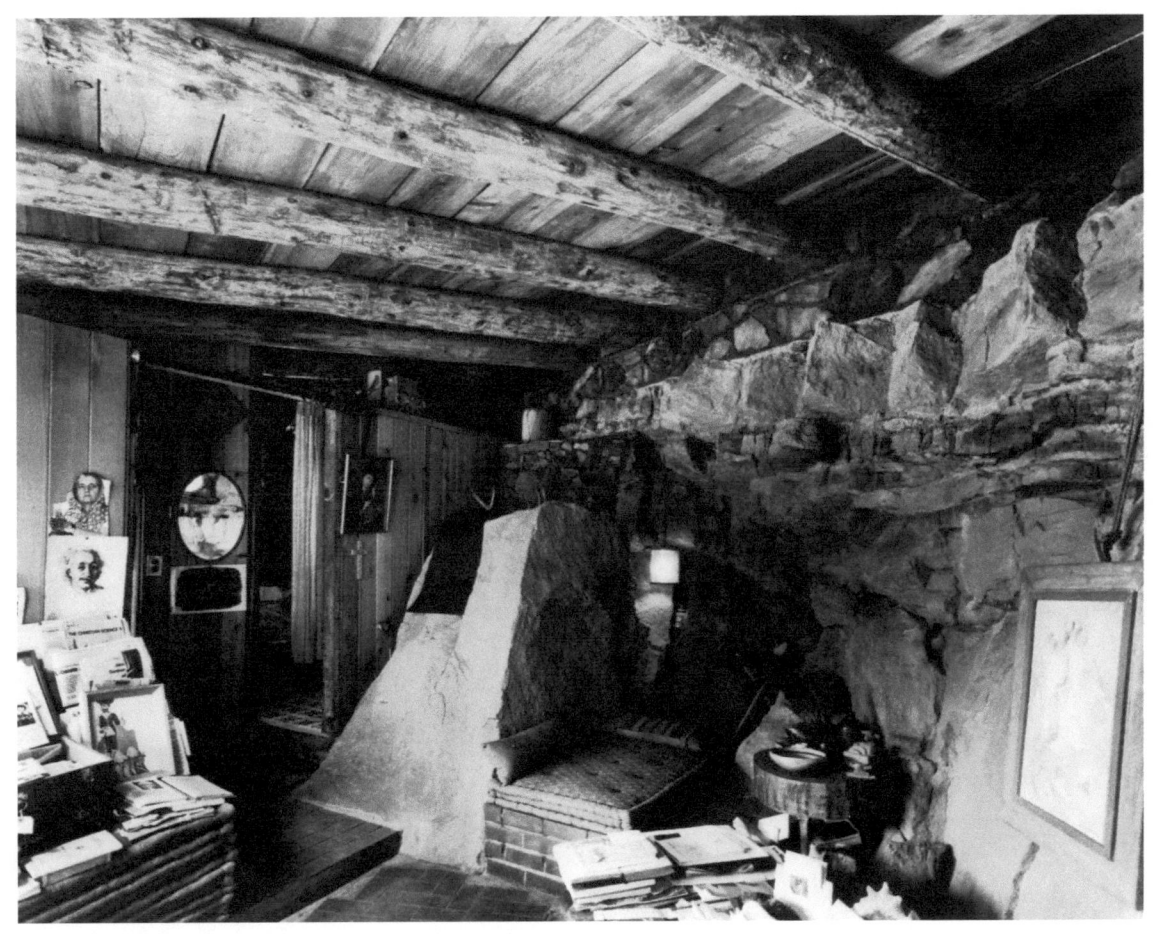

TOWER HOUSE

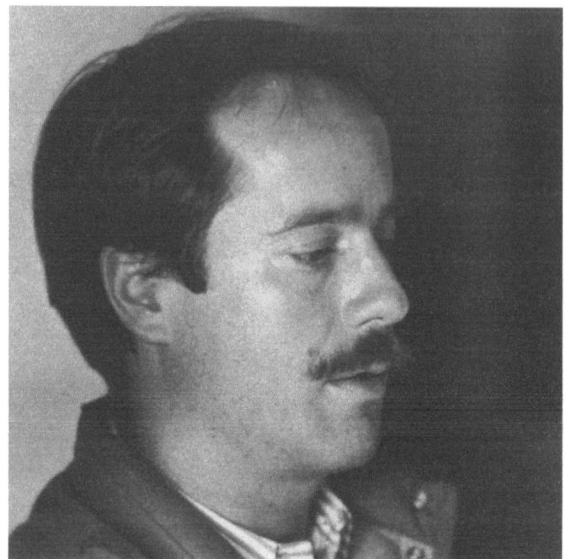

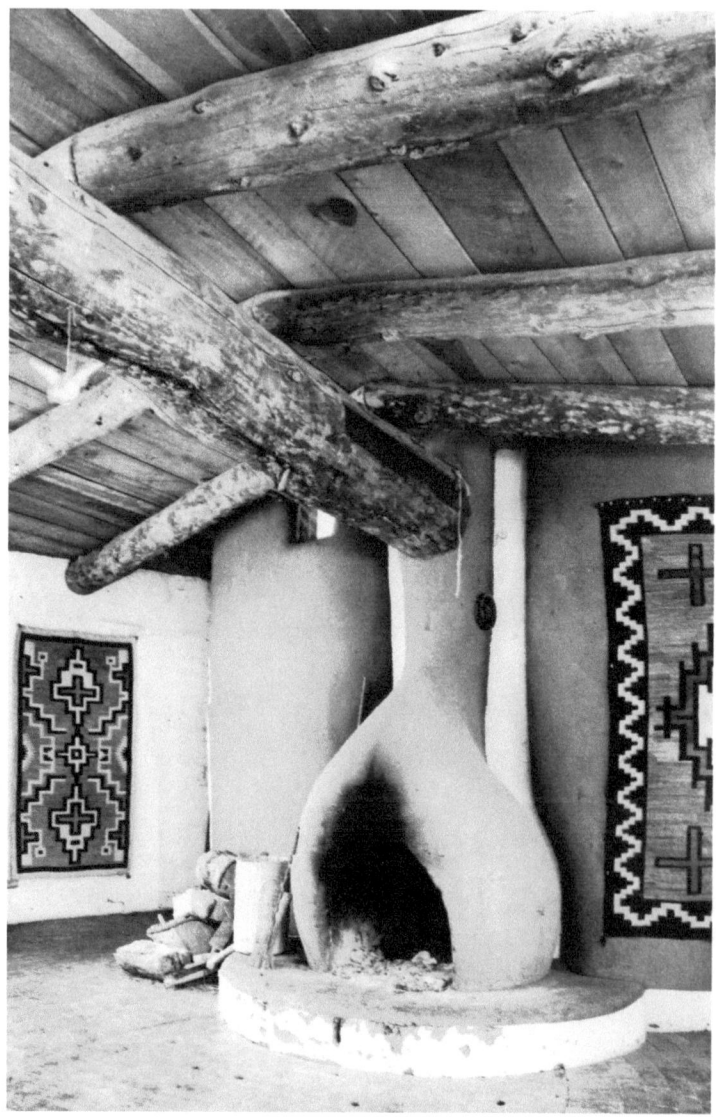

HAL: I was an artist in the city until I moved to Colorado where I saw so many people building beautiful houses, doing amazing things. I decided to try building myself, so I started with a split-level cabin, followed by a small A-frame. Then I came to New Mexico and built my first adobe.

In 1972 HAL *and* CANDY MIGEL *undertook a more ambitious project—a large, complex house with many curving walls and hallways connecting two-story towers. It took them and a full-time crew a year to build. They, and their three children, moved in before the house was completely finished.*

HAL: It was easier for me to build that house since I'd had a lot of visual experience and knew what I wanted. We had a floor plan and a couple of elevations, yet some things had to be worked out as we went along. When

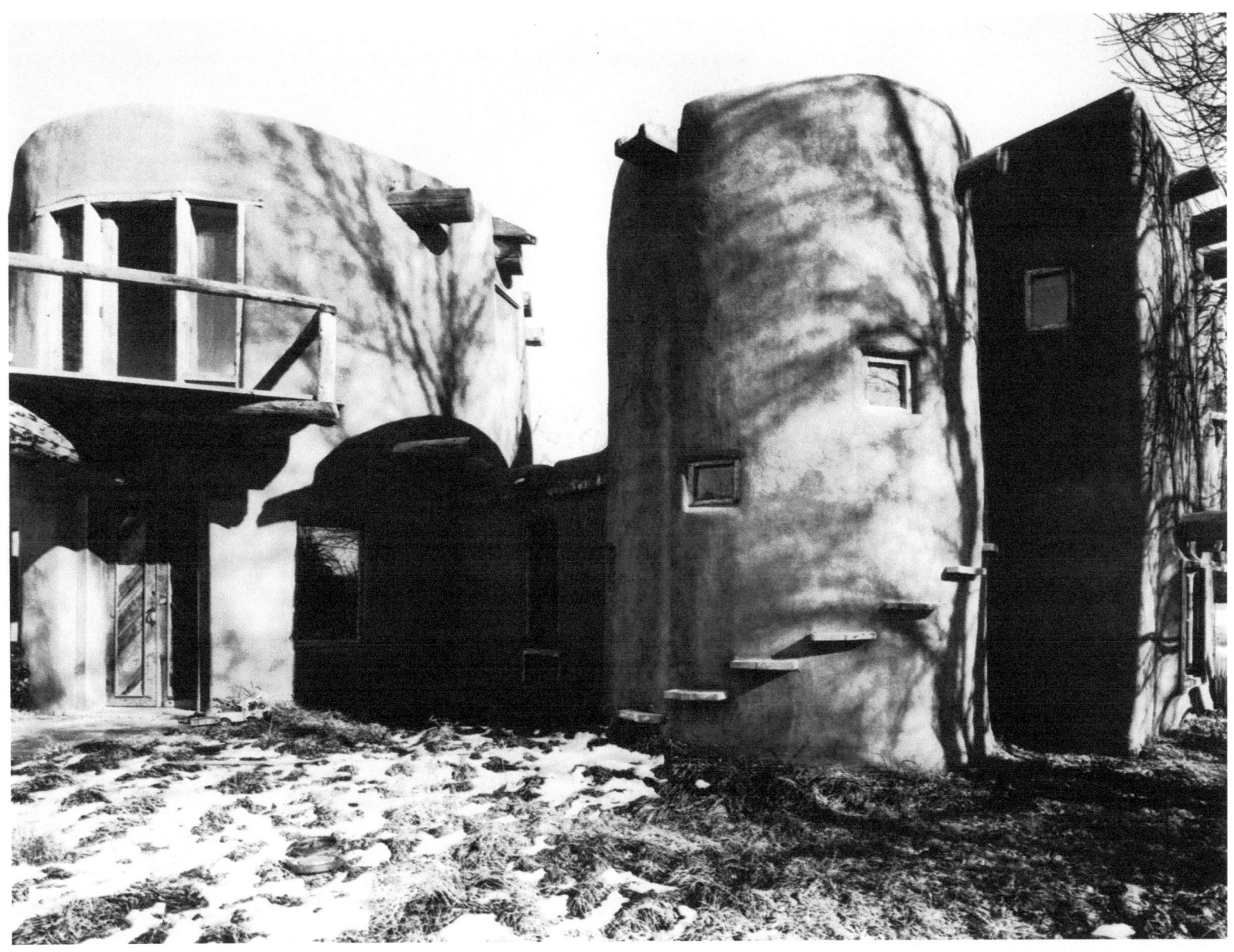

you live in a house while you're building it, each time you add a detail, paint a stripe around a doorway, you become part of its growth.

CANDY: It was huge, like a castle, yet very natural. It fulfilled all those wish-dreams we had as kids—of bedrooms in trees with hammocks and birds singing out. It's something I now know I can have any time, any place; can re-create again and again. I know where to find it—it's part of me.

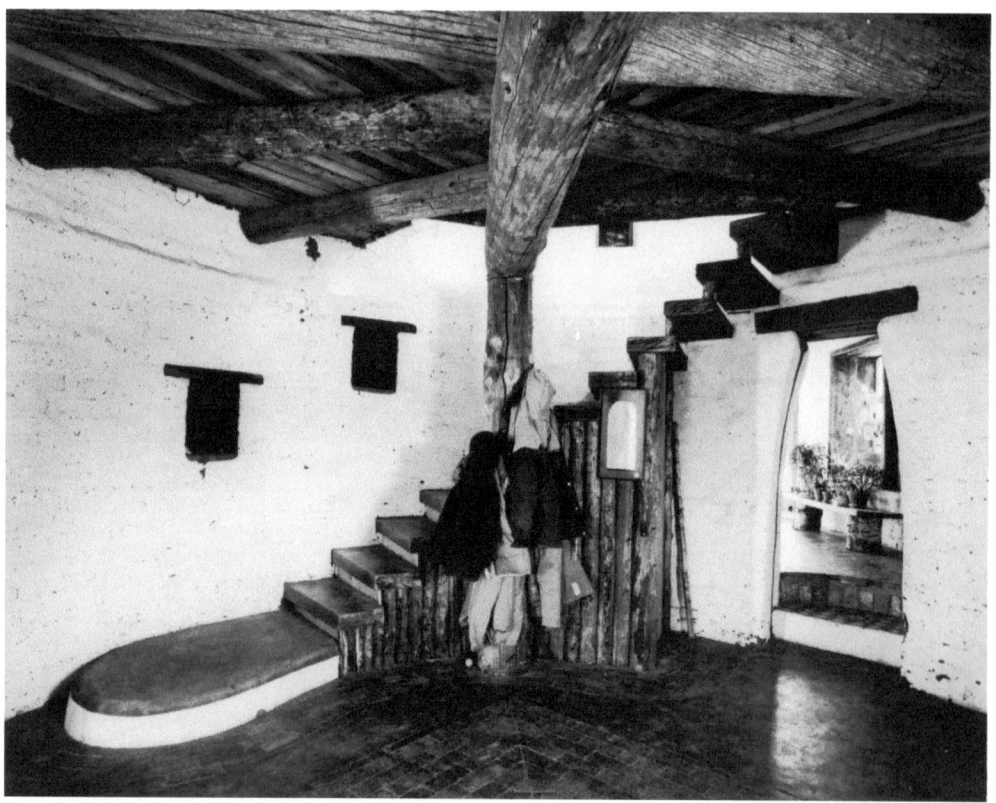

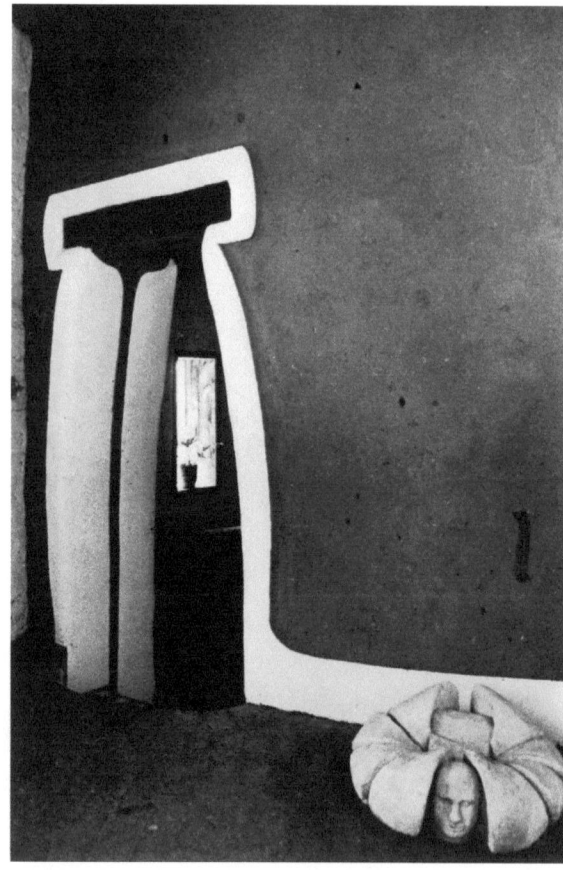

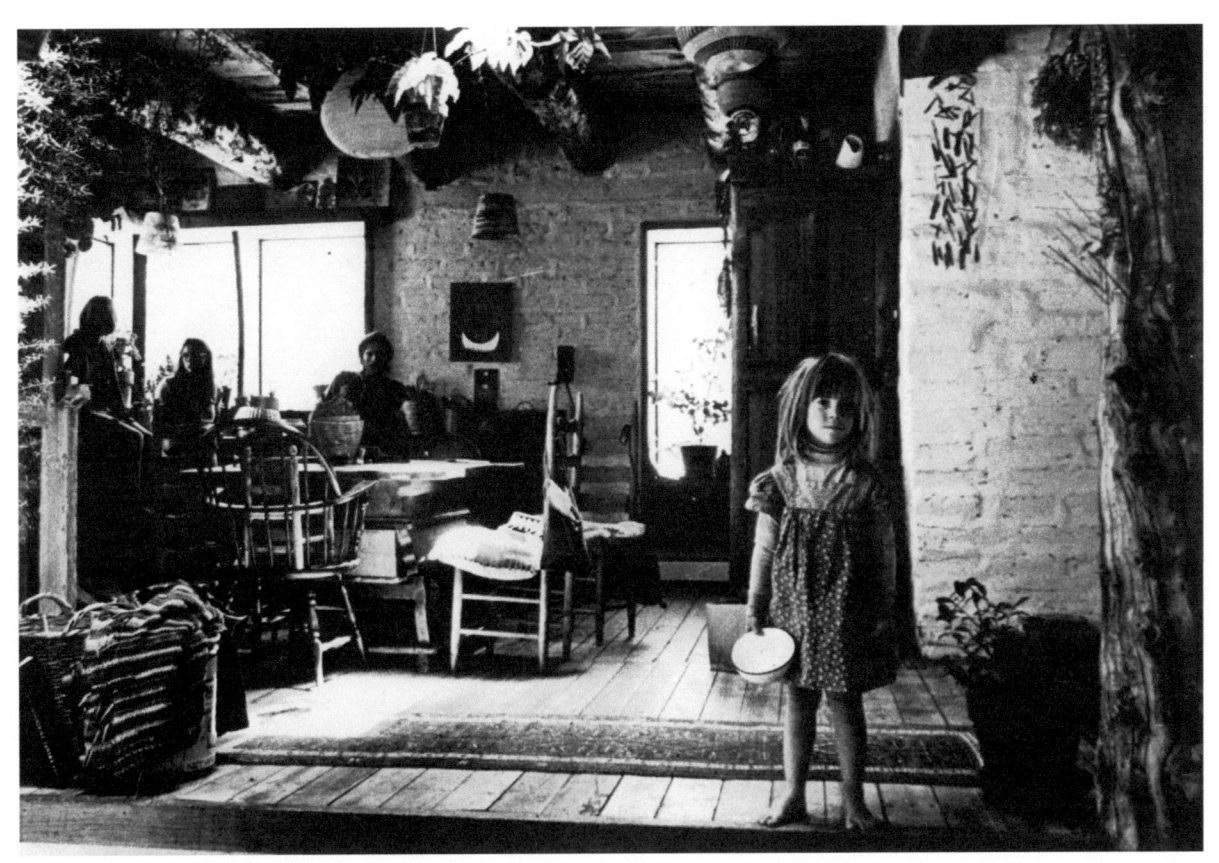

SUN PILLOW

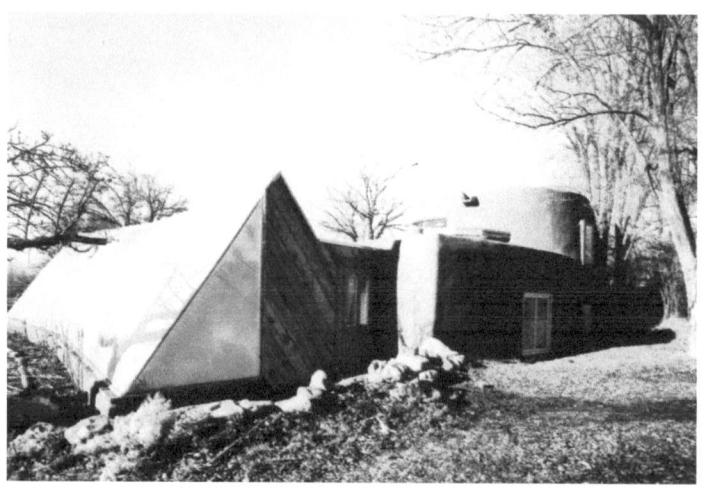

In 1974 Hal and Candy sold that house and built a smaller, sun-powered house nextdoor. They moved in the following March.

HAL: I'm a total convert to solar energy. I still believe that building as an art form can be more real than the so-called fine arts; I've just added another system over the esthetic one. My work now is designing and building solar houses.

CANDY: The other house was too large and hard to keep clean. I'm more comfortable in smaller spaces.

HAL: The greenhouse, facing south, is constructed of two layers of polyethelene sheeting; a fan blows air between the layers, inflating them. It's the only way to use plastic on a large scale for windows. The system is called a sun pillow, and in the wind acts as a pneumatic cushion. Once a dust devil flattened the garden fence. I was afraid it would demolish the greenhouse too, but when the dust devil hit, the greenhouse survived beautifully—it just billowed and flexed.

The heat in the greenhouse is pushed by another fan through a layer of three-inch river rocks stored under the floor that charge the whole house with radiant heat. The house walls are a mix of pumice and adobe poured

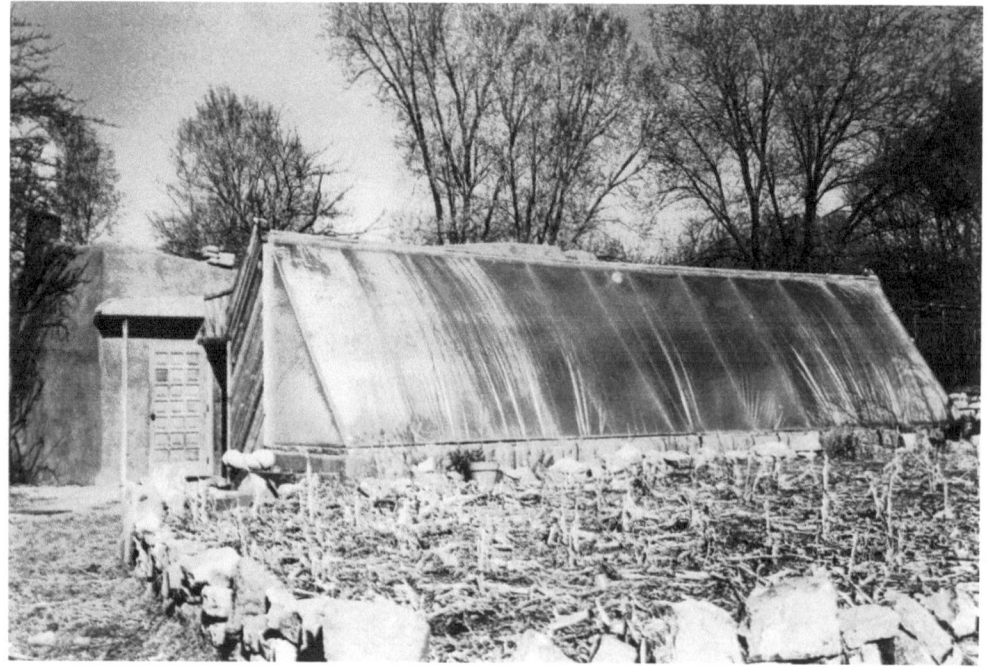

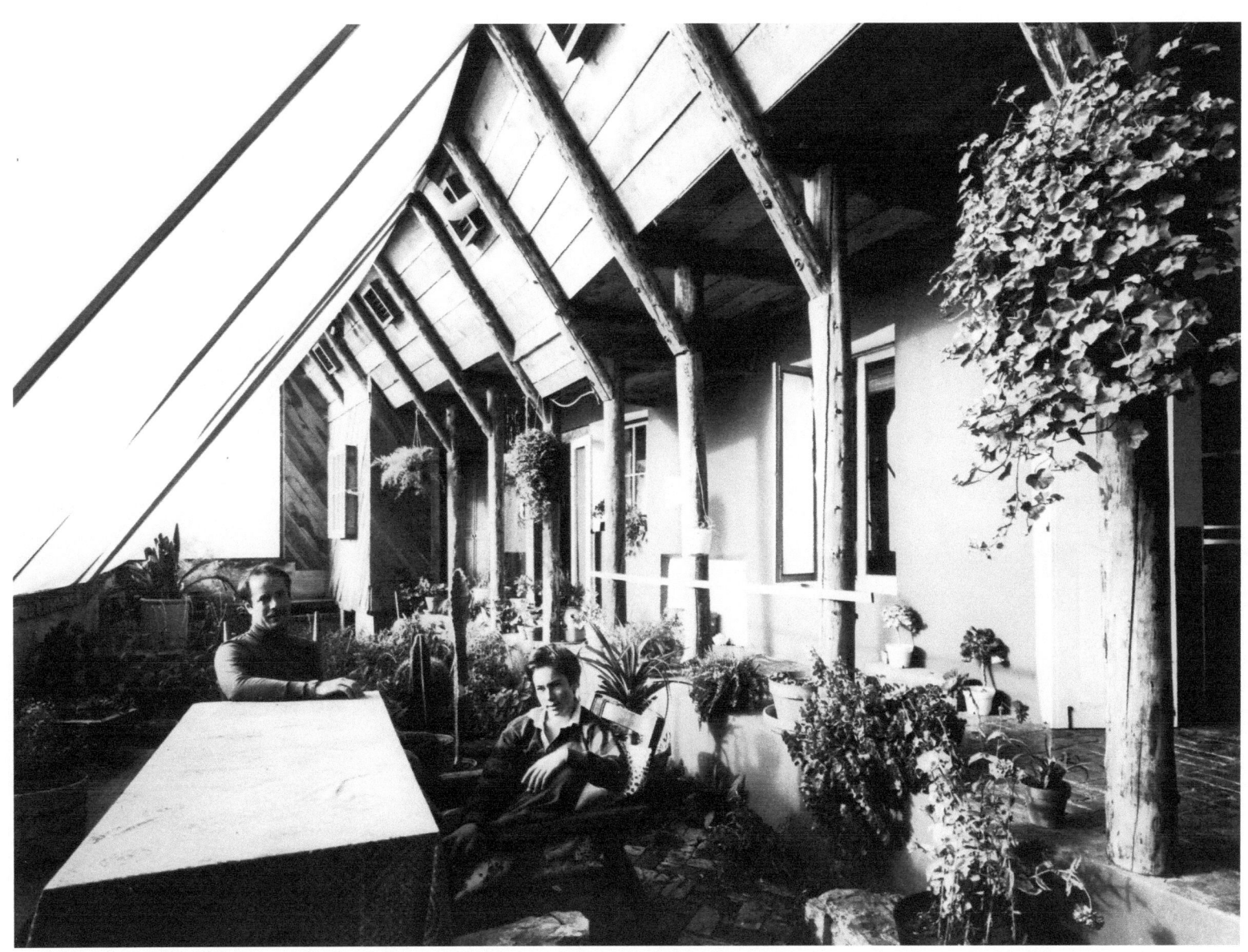

twenty four inches thick which I call a direct earth cast. With two inches of plastic insulation on the outside, the house is like a huge thermal flywheel. We just keep pushing heat in and it never gets cold. There's a back-up system, but we rarely need it.

Building this house was an intense experience. No one had worked on a building like this and I got contradictory advice from engineers. There I was, spending my money and left to make my own decisions.

Living in the house now, I run it like a boat—I keep a trim ship. I adjust the speed of the fans and regulate the air flow. I monitor everything because I want to build systems like this for other people. It fits right in with redefining life-styles, living patterns and utilizing natural energy sources.

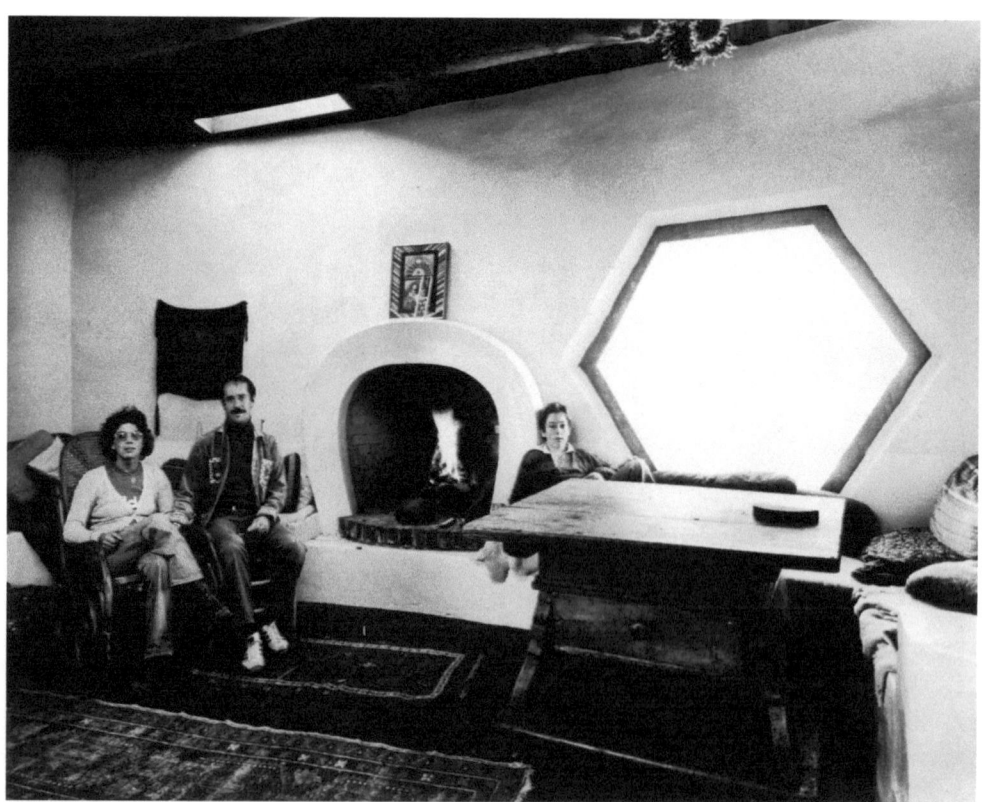

FIREPLACES

THE EARLY SOUTHWESTERN Indian fireplace was simply a firepit in the floor with a hole in the ceiling to draw off the smoke. In the early 1600s Spanish explorers, with their Mediterranean heritage, introduced the more structured fireplace. Built in a corner, it had a simple smoke-gathering hood with a tapering flue through the roof. Sometimes the hood was extended and this shelf was used to dry food and was also a warm place to sleep—the shepherd's fireplace. In some instances a short wall was built at a right angle to a main wall, creating a corner for a fireplace.

Today even the most unconventional adobe homes have at least one fireplace. Some owners continue the tradition of building a fireplace in every room. Fireplaces are a cheerful source of heat and serve as gathering places for the rooms they warm.

These fireplaces are also personal expressions, for adobe's malleable qualities allow the creation of a sculptural form to embrace the primal attraction of the open fire.

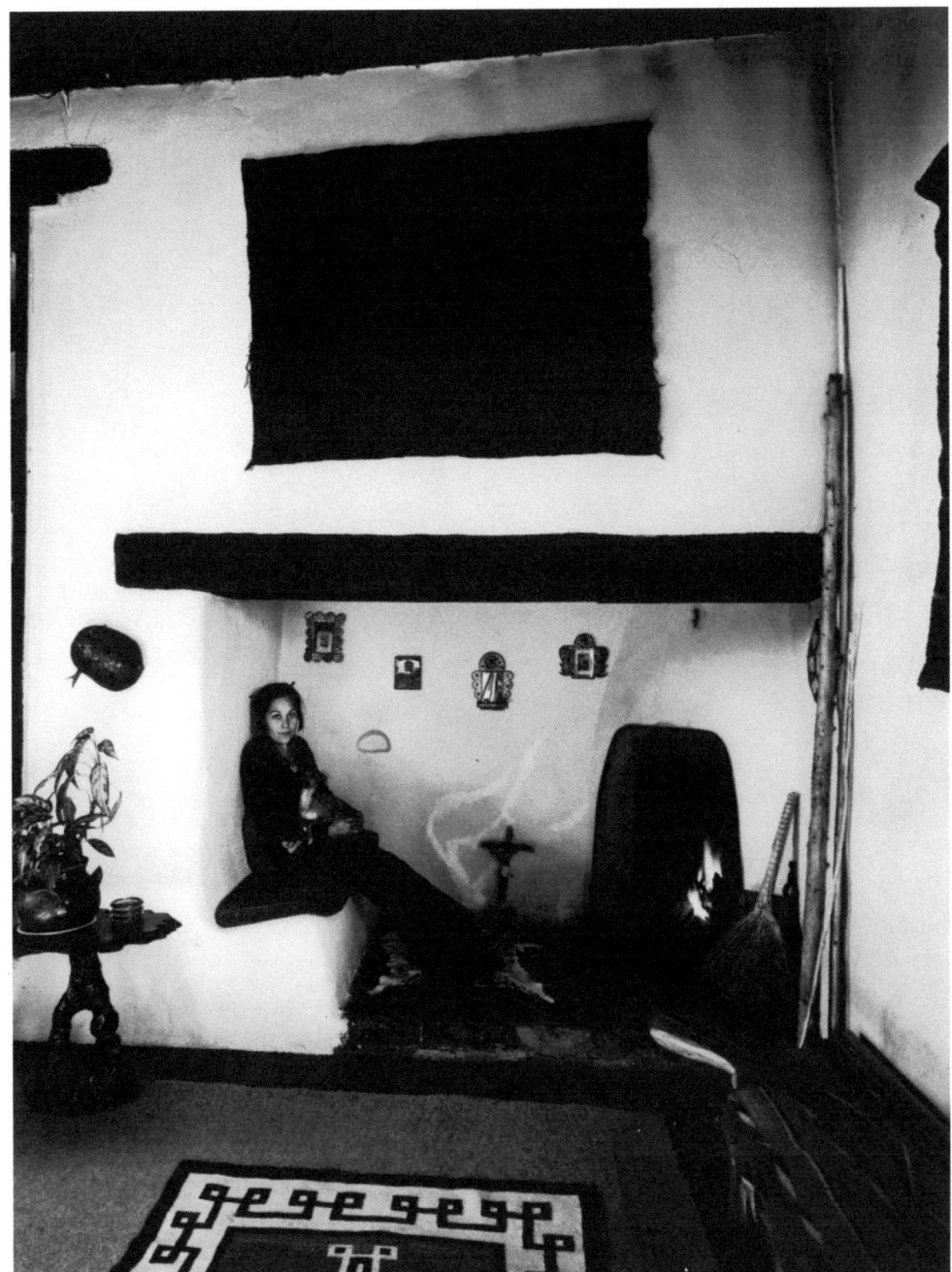

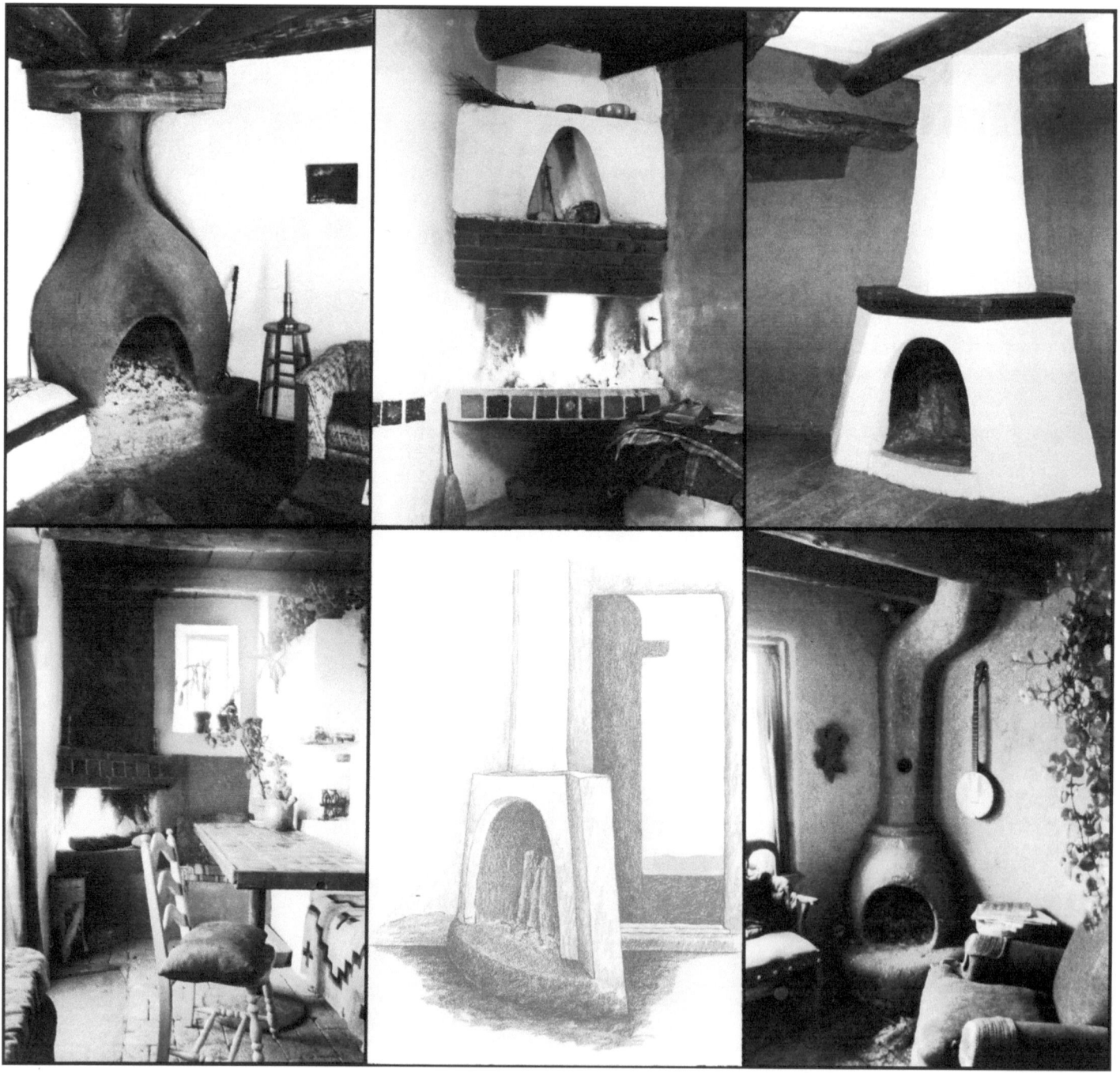

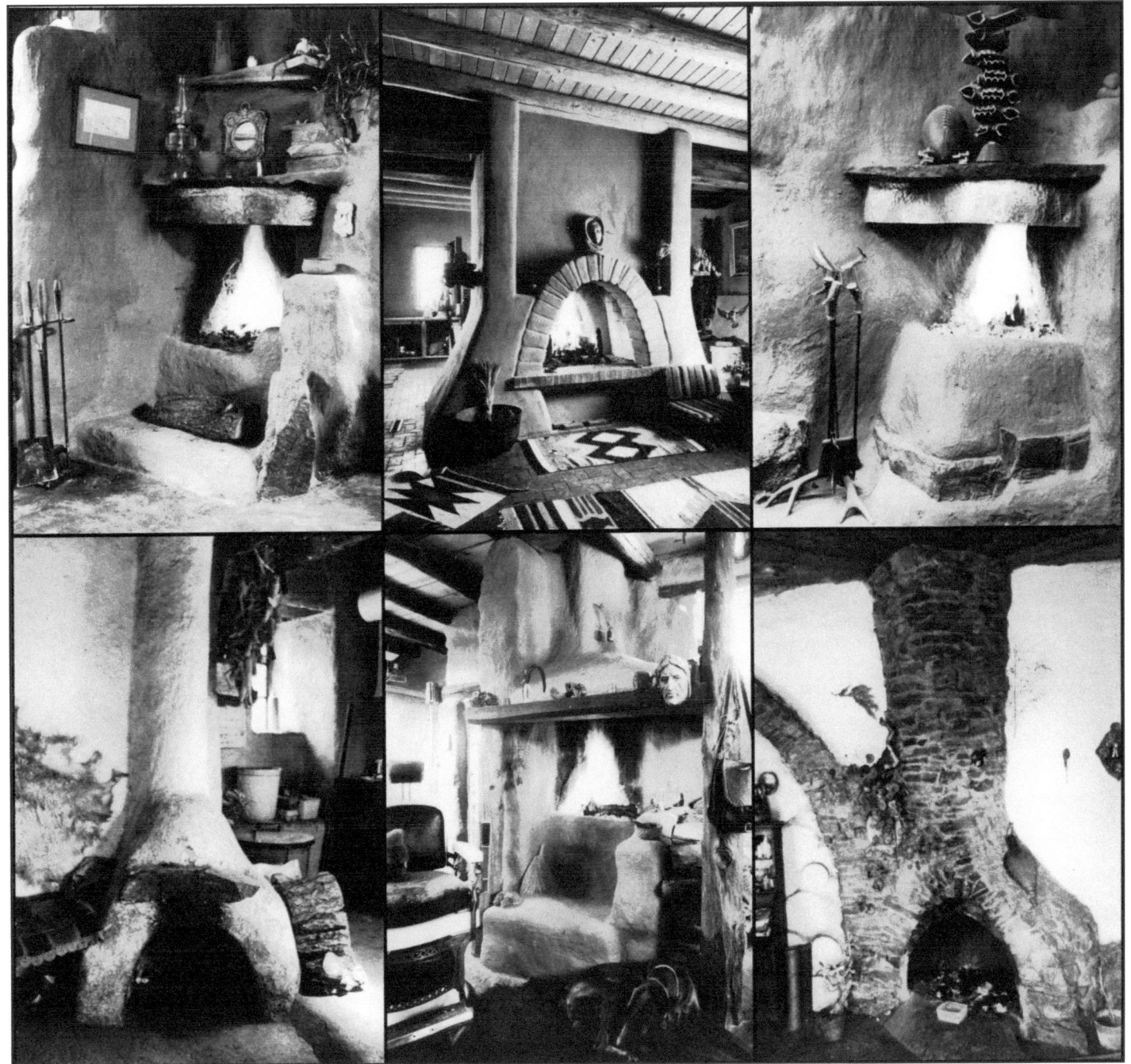

43

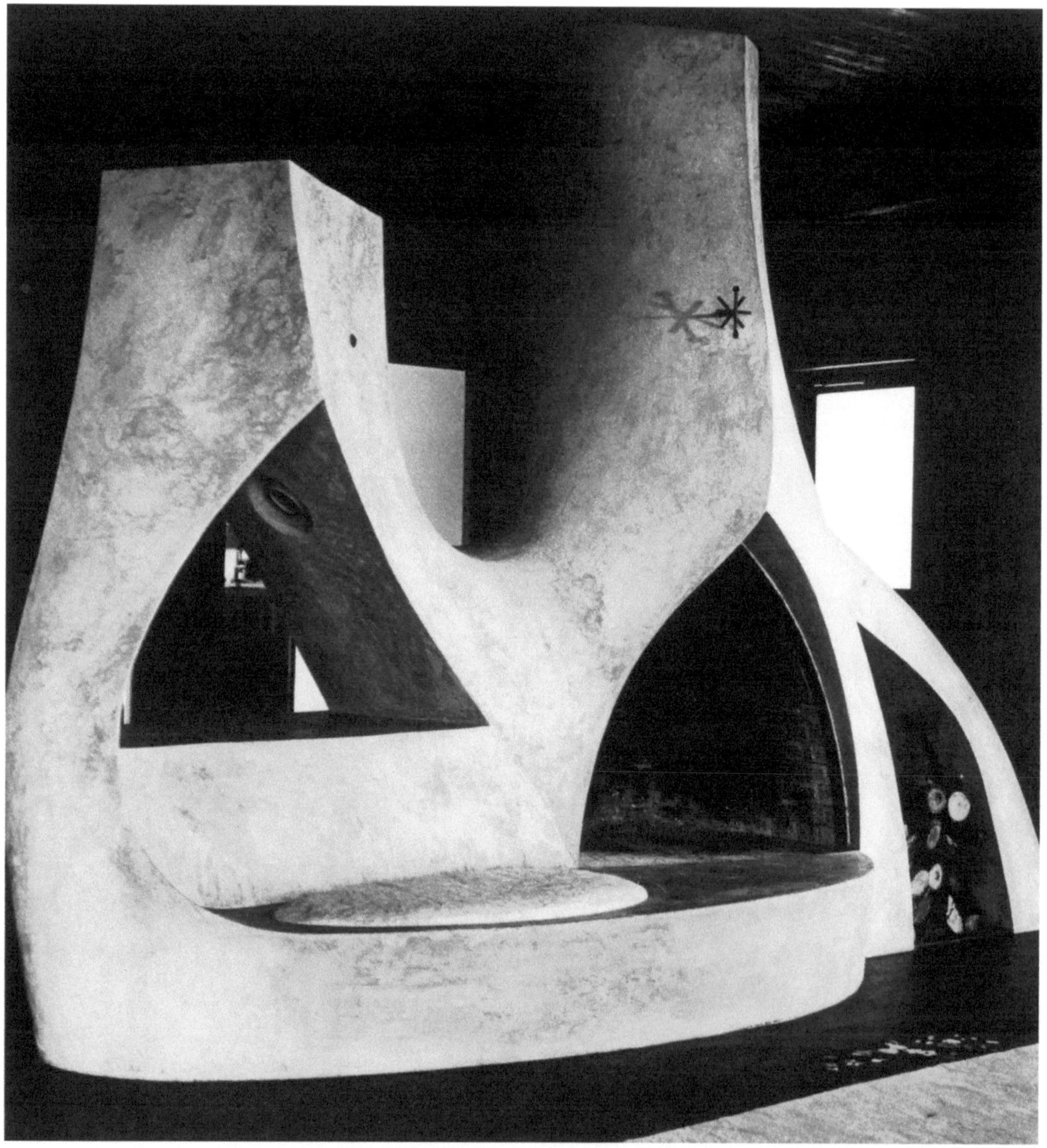

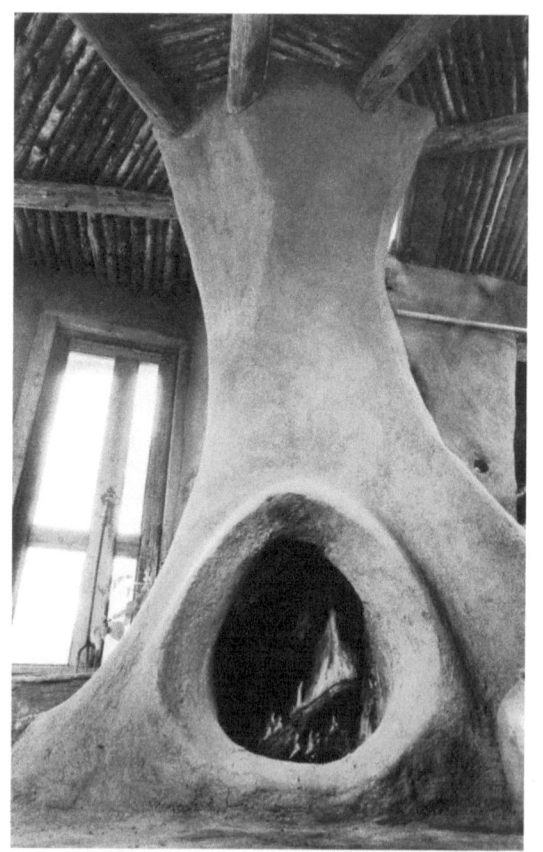

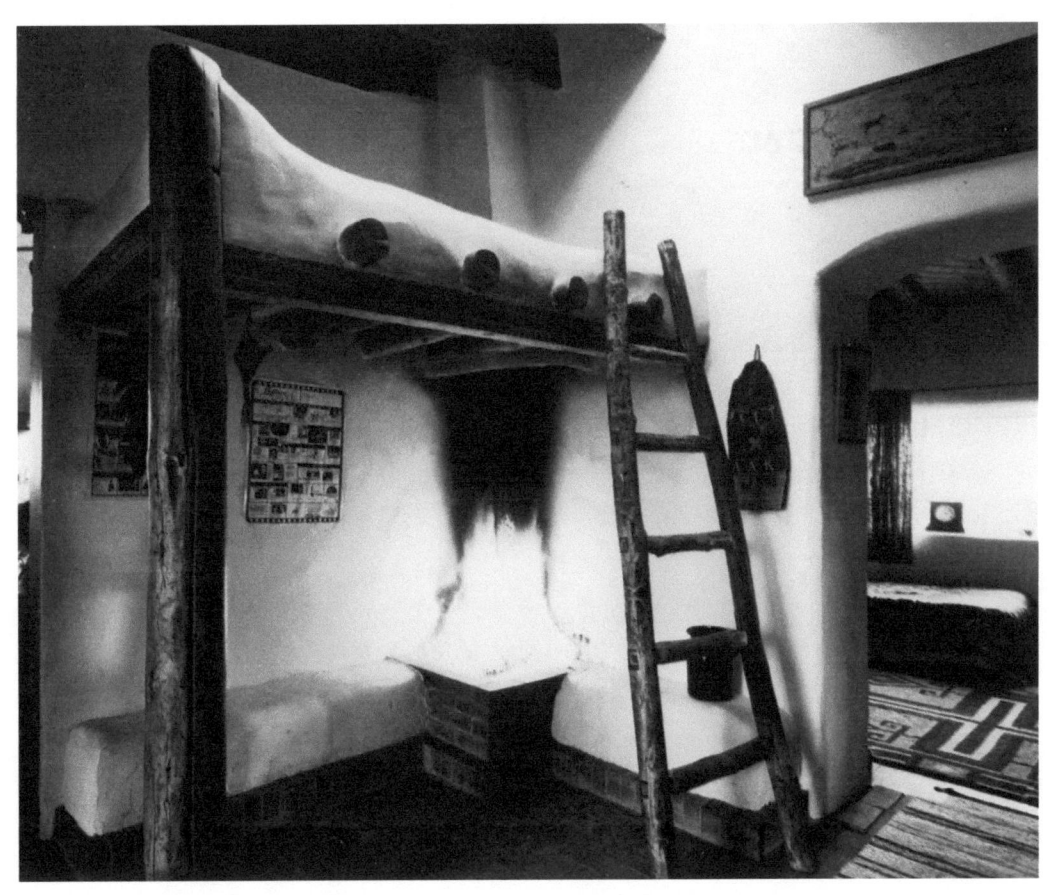

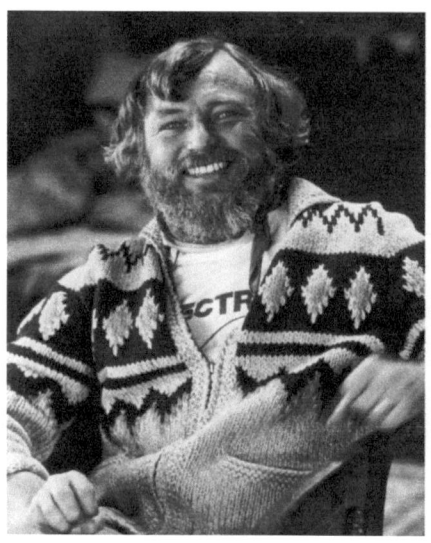 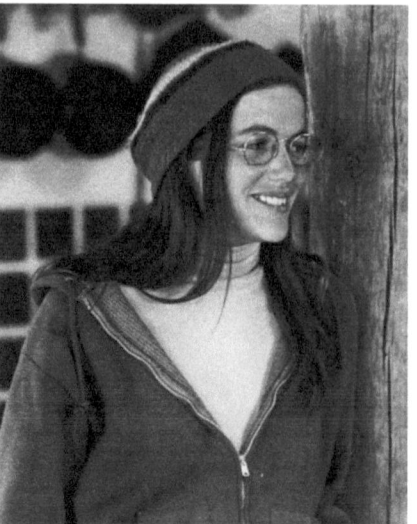

RAINBOW HOUSE

JACK: Santa Fe is fantastically old. It was an Indian pueblo long before the Spanish came. This canyon is a holy place to me. It gives birth to this particular town; the canyon and river come right out of the mountains.

JACK LOEFFLER and KATHY STRAIN bought land from a friend in 1973. A large house had been planned and all the foundations poured before they took over. They used a third of the footings and lived nearby in a small tent during the summer they built.

JACK: A house is a primordial urge that resolves itself into concrete form. We looked at the original plans long and hard. A large house had been designed and there were several possibilities, different sections from which to choose. We wanted a big room, as large as possible, so we picked what was to have been the garage. Then a smaller space

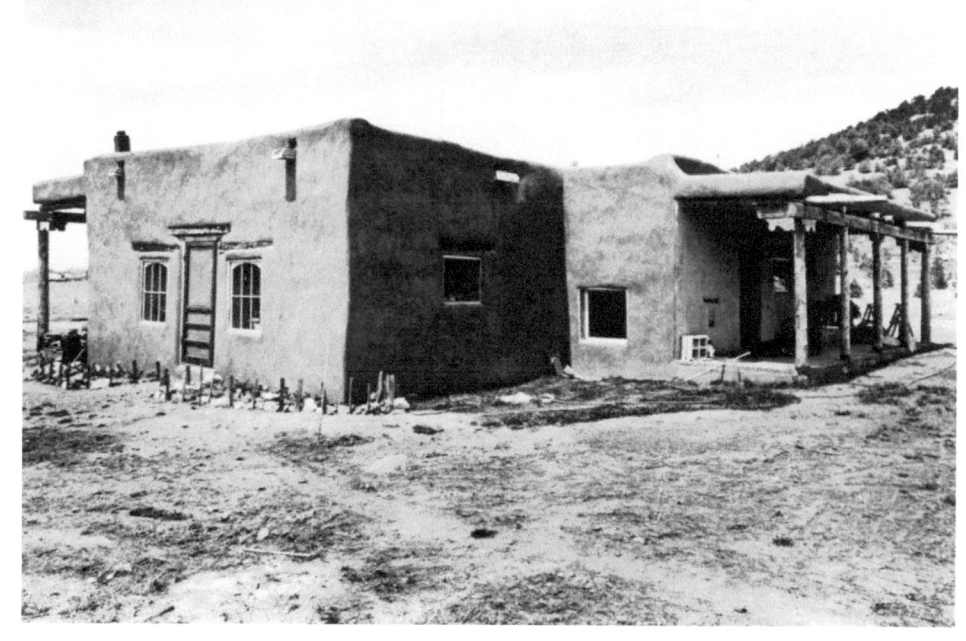

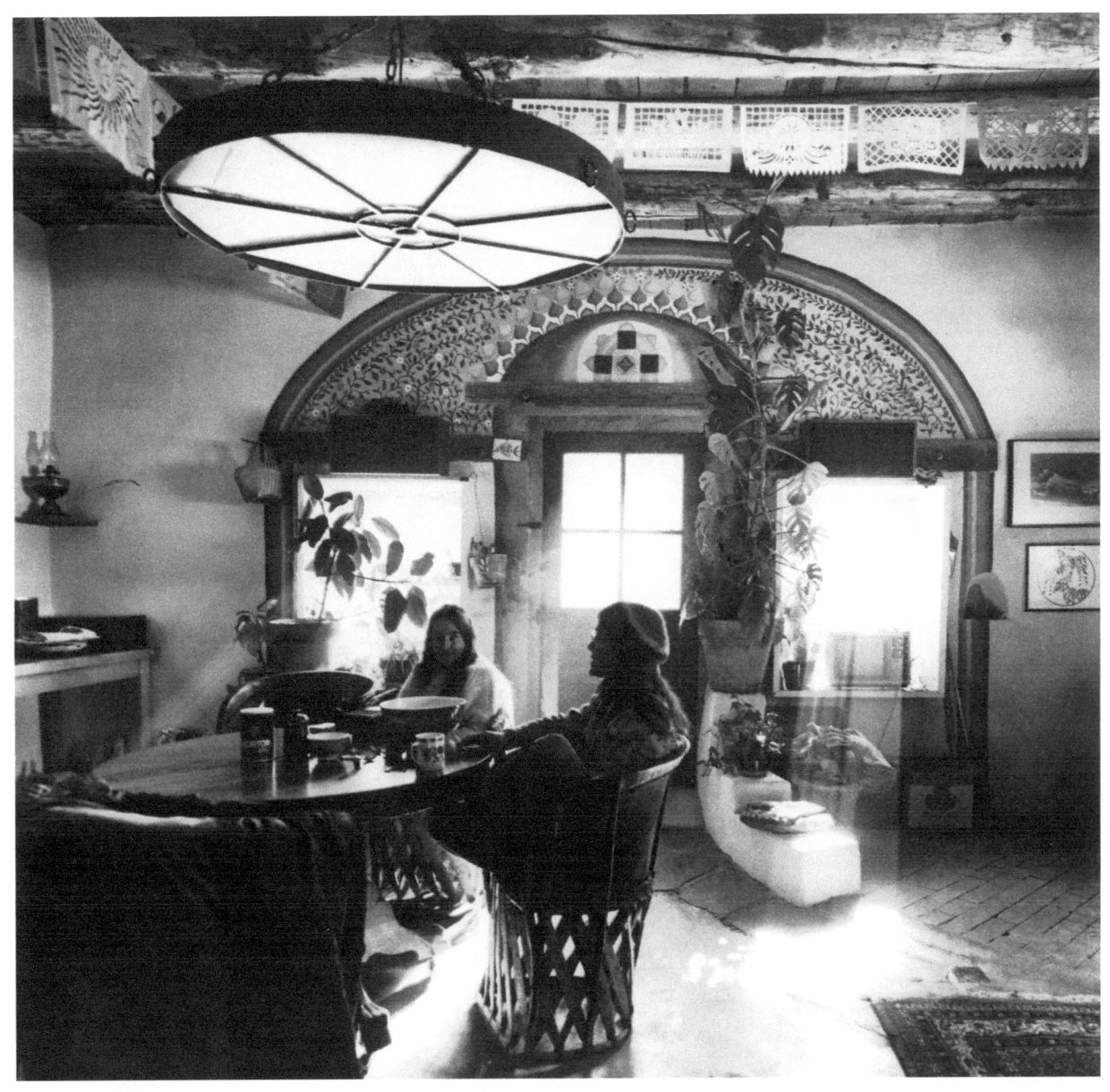

for the bedroom. The rest of the footings are still out there in the field.

KATHY: We worked one step at a time, gathering the materials ourselves. We didn't know much about building, but friends helped us. We hired a back-hoe to hoist the vigas onto the walls. When the back-hoe man arrived friends came from everywhere to help. There were eight guys on top of the walls risking their lives. By the time the bond beam and the vigas were up, the ceiling was two feet higher than we had planned.

JACK: I don't mind the sacrifice in heat because there's room for my thoughts to soar.

Kathy did much of the carpentry and finishing inside. Around windows and doors she painted rainbows and other multi-colored designs suggestive of American Indian art.

KATHY: I wish I had a whole new room, so I could do more.

This house is uniquely situated: the state capitol is two miles in one direction and the wilderness is two miles in the other.

JACK: I live now in a very civilized fashion compared to the way I used to live. But I'd say I'm about half as perceptive as when I'm living outdoors. My awareness is much greater when I'm out in the boondocks.

KATHY: When you relate to the house every day, your focus really narrows. Since we built it ourselves, there's a real attachment. This has become our commitment, our roots.

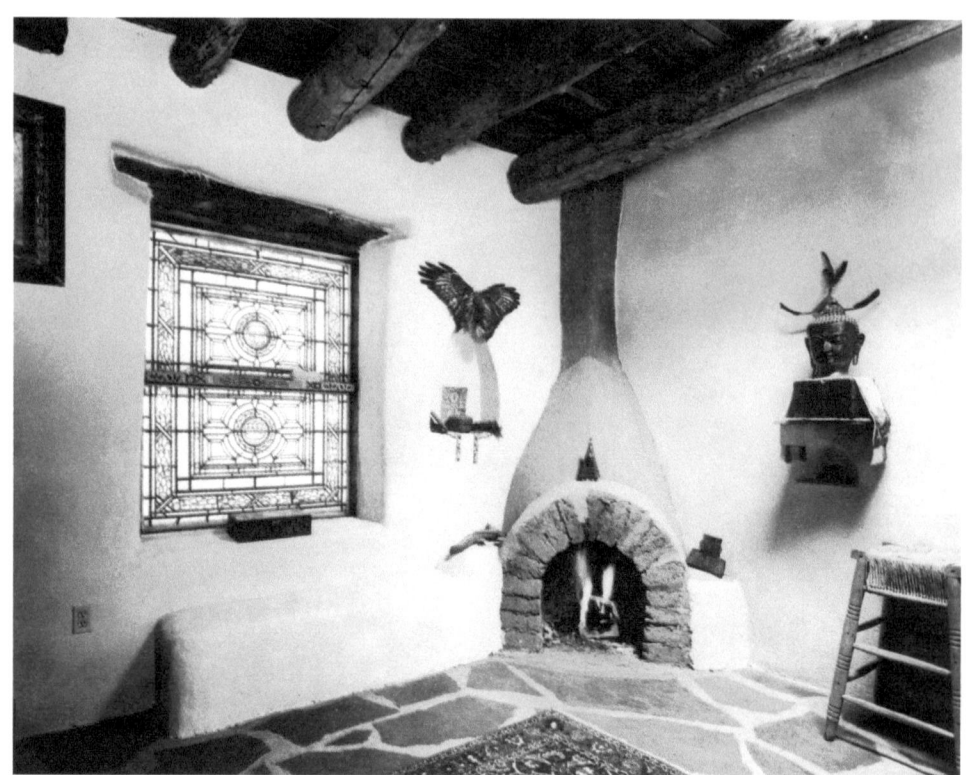

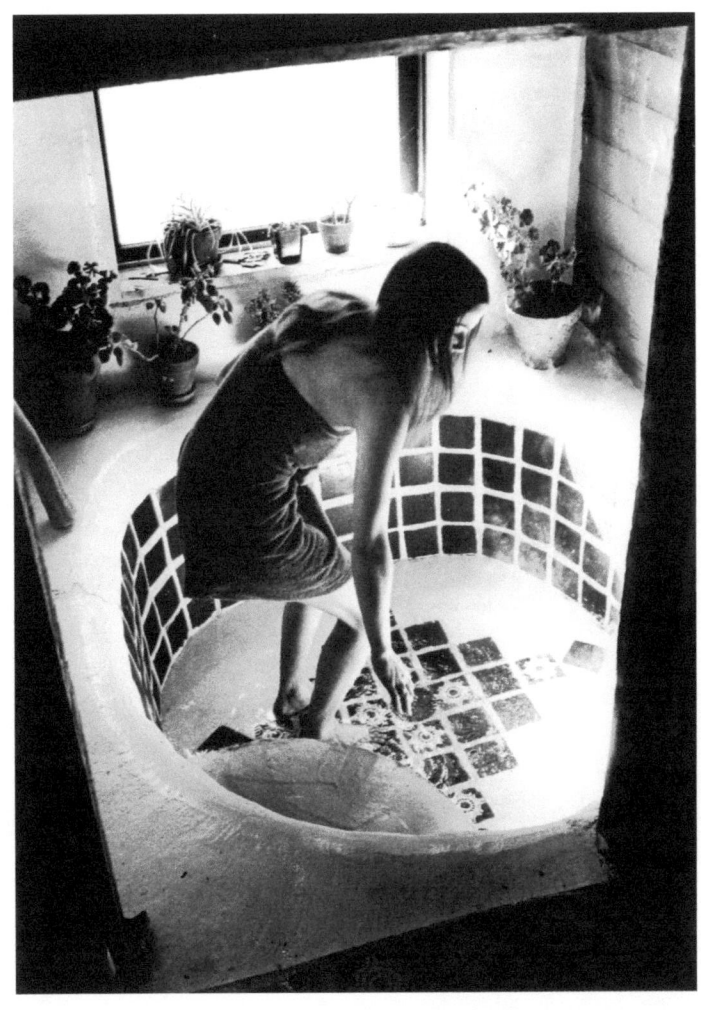
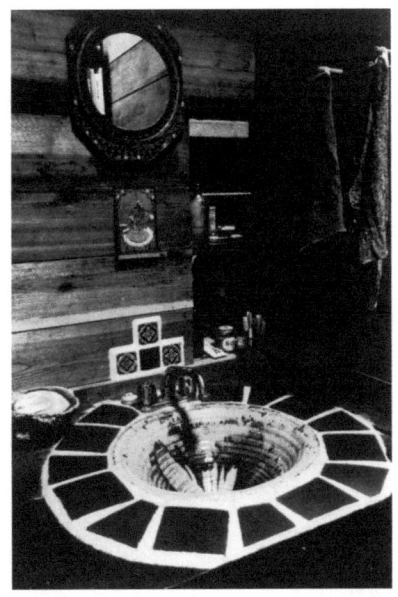
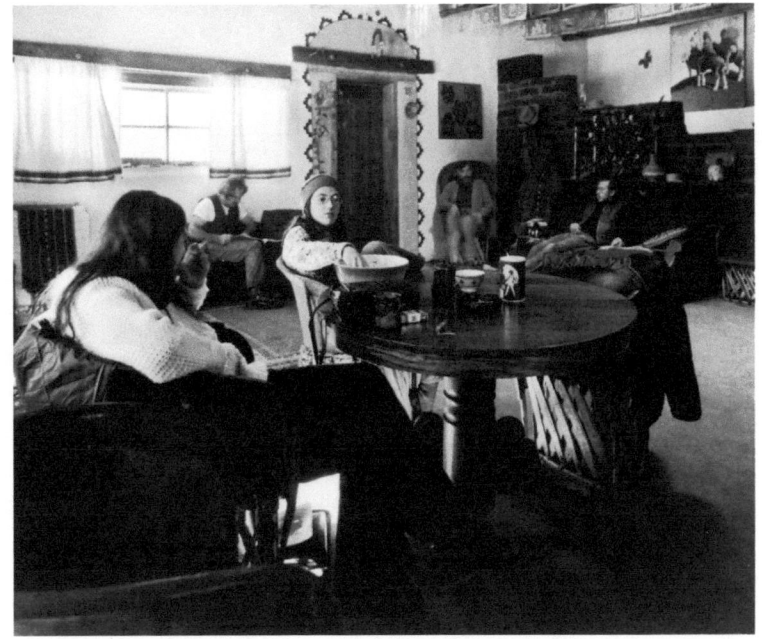

OPEN HOUSE

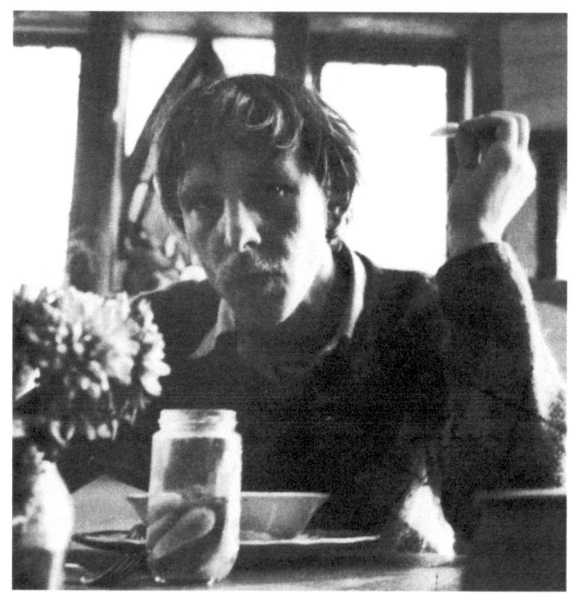

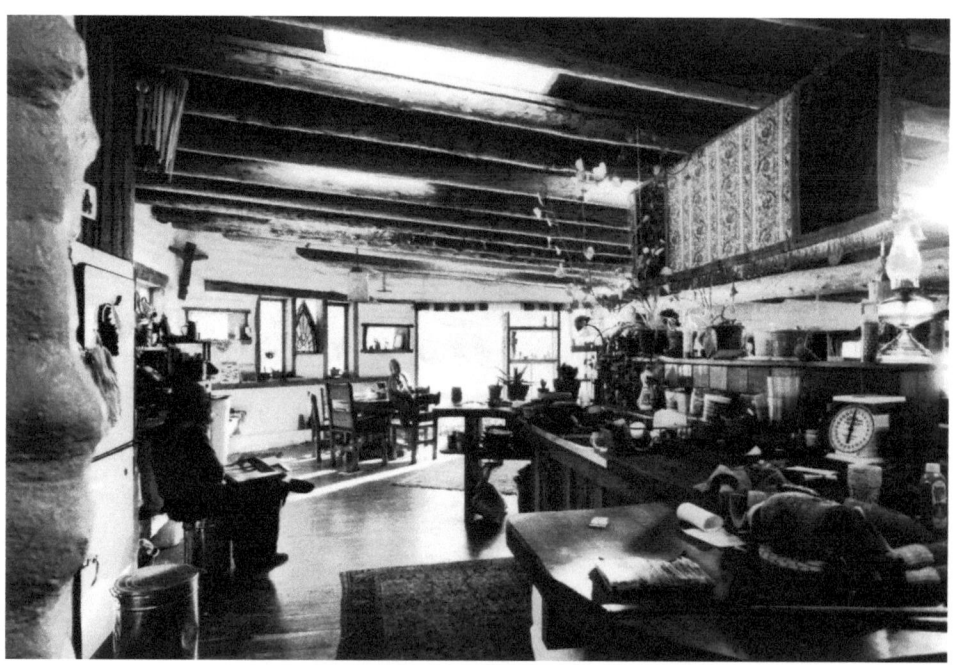

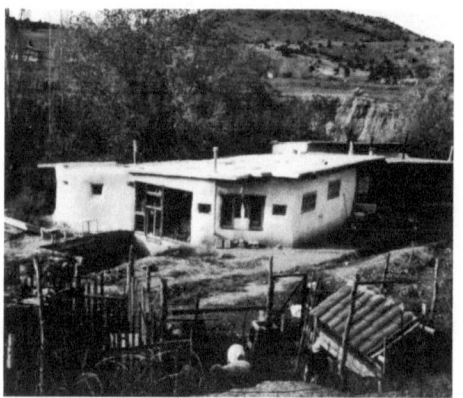

JOHN MARCH, *who makes his living laying tile, bought some country land with a storage shed on it. He lived there four months while he added on a large room. It's now a household that includes John, wife Judy, and three small children.*

JOHN: With the space the way it is, everybody's on top of each other; somebody's cooking, somebody's watching television, somebody's trying to read, but it works fine. The interaction is good, even the friction you get is all right. People need human contact.

I don't like homes where living is compartmentalized. Sometimes a lack of imagination designs too much solitude and privacy into our lives. Homes should be built with relationships in mind, rather than unused spaces: living rooms like parlors, dining rooms waiting for the next yearly banquet. Here I can wash dishes and listen to television without it being in the kitchen.

Since building the big room in 1971 John and Judy have added two rooms: a small bedroom for themselves, and another for the kids.

JUDY: I like the big room as it is, but I'm eager to see it broken up a bit more. The kids need their own space. I don't see this as a contradiction, but as an affirmation of the individual within the family where each person has a place to himself and still shares the family space.

John and Judy, with help of friends, did the building at very low cost.

JOHN: The bedroom was built from salvaged materials. I made the adobe bricks right on the wall; poured the mud into forms, pulled off the forms, and just waited until the next time I felt like doing a round. It cost nothing but my labor and when I'm working for myself it's the job that counts. I don't see it as a sacrifice of earning power.

Judy is a weaver who works at home.

JUDY: At one point I didn't want my studio attached to the house. I wanted it completely separate, but that's impossible since I'm also a housekeeper. I have to make meals and I can't keep running back and forth. But with the studio in the house I can run over and save the soup from burning.

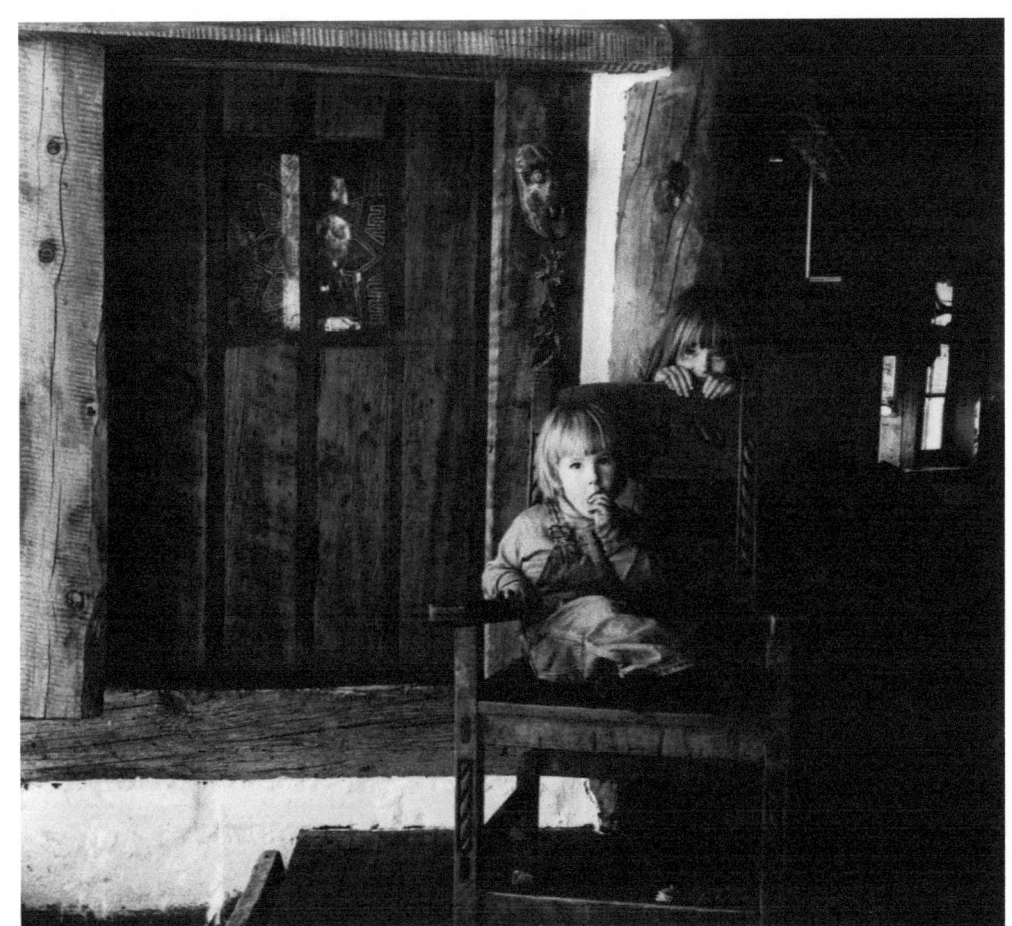

ADRIENNE: This is a pushing out house, on many levels. The whole thing is very symbolic. It records our changes.

NICK *and* ADRIENNE'S *is a large house dug into the side of a gentle slope, mostly underground. The southern area is a greenhouse about twenty by thirty feet with a small meditation room off to one side. Nick is a potter and jeweler and also studied architecture.*

NICK: The idea is to build spaces we can live in that fit into nature: using the sun for heating, using growholes and light sources to collect natural heat as well as bringing plant life into the human indoor environment. Natural materials are important for the vibratory enclosure they offer. Living with stone, wood and clay can be expansive to growing things. Be careful, however, that these materials don't create a great cleaning problem. Surfaces that collect dust filter out as many vibrations as synthetic materials.

The space that most complements our higher self and solves our physical needs is different for all of us. May each of you find yours and share it with your brothers.

ADRIENNE: My plan was to live in a greenhouse. I wanted living quarters and greenhouse together. Nick started with little modules of the way we live and move inside a house.

We started in 1972. The first year we did nothing but gather materials. A lot of people came to apprentice pottery with Nick and got

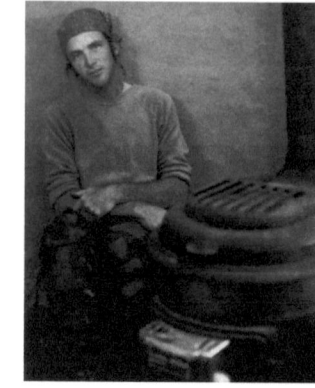
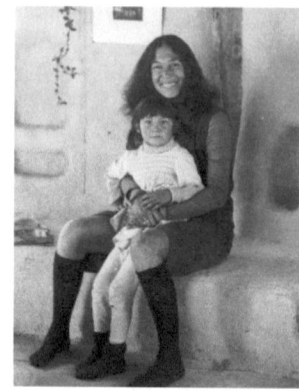

GROWHOLE

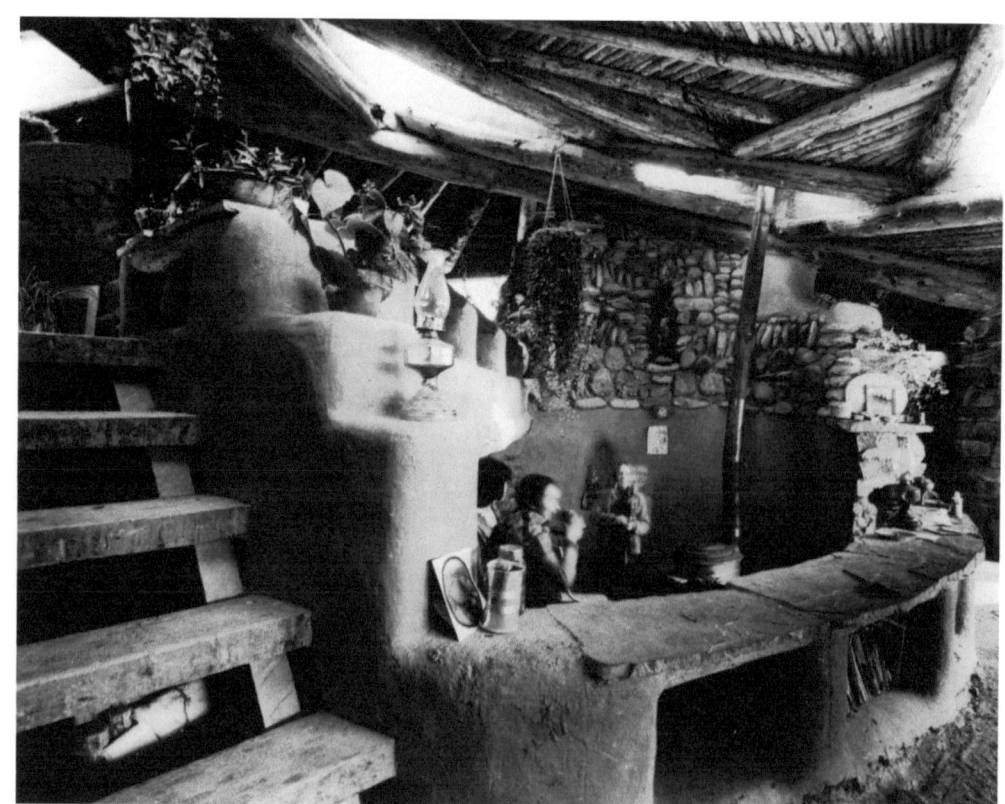

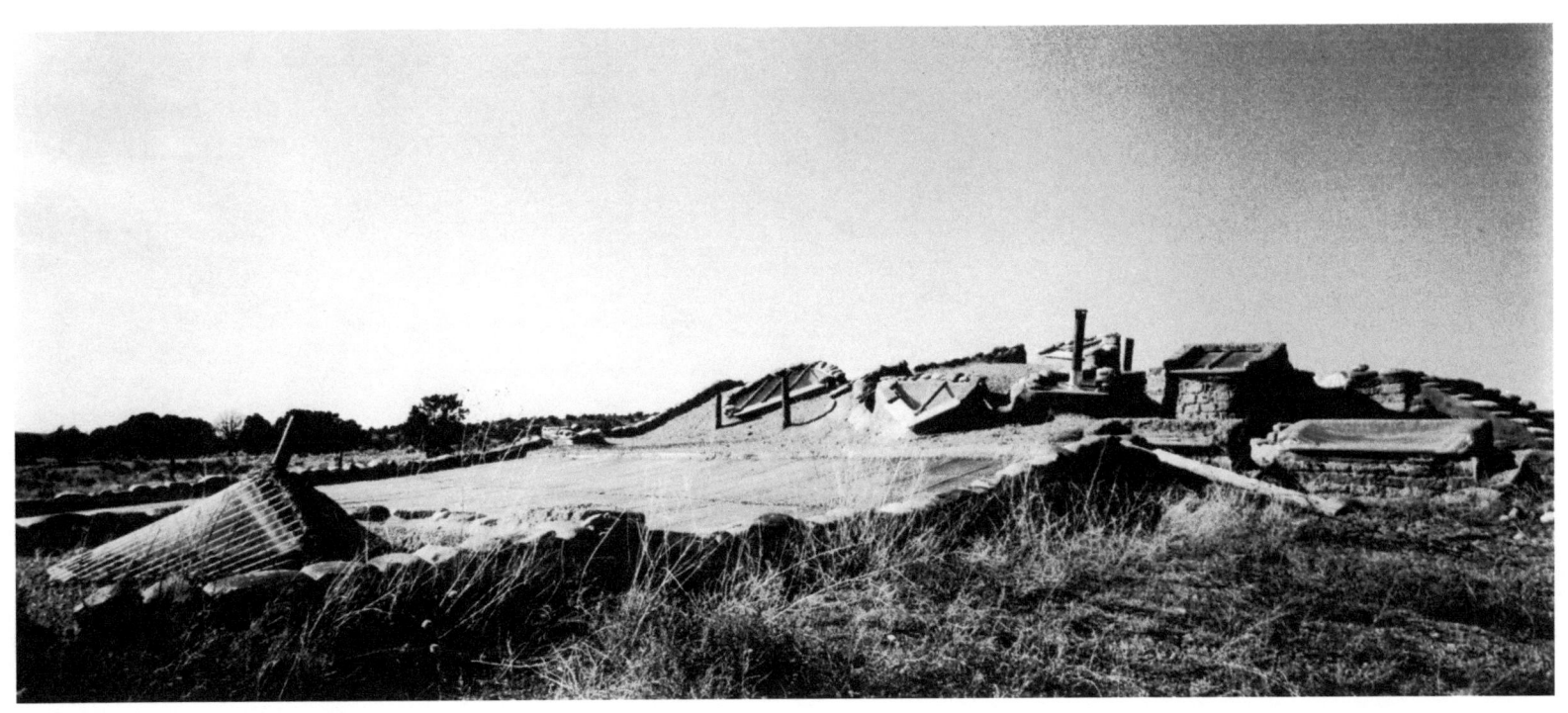

drawn into the building from their own enthusiasm. We didn't have much money to hire people, so it was "Come stay, we'll feed you and you help us."

None of us had any idea how the house would look. Nick would tell us what the next day's work was going to be. At that time four people lived with us who formed the nucleus of the crew. What we all felt about the house was important, so Nick would bring up a plan and we'd all discuss it. That's the way it happened; nothing on paper. It just evolved.

It was an incredible amount of emotional work. It seems spacious now, but when all of us were living here our need for privacy was immense. Then Nick and I had some confrontations, because I'd look at the house and say, "It's nothing like we discussed—how come?" But now I see it's very much what I I was feeling and talking about.

This is almost a rock house. We started by using flat rock from way over in Ski Valley, then began gathering these nice friendly round stones right here in the gully. But I'm telling you I fought tooth and nail for any adobe that's in here.

I was born in New Mexico and have an innate feeling for mud. We were born around mud and as kids we'd play at what we saw the grown-ups doing. Being a native I'm the one who always says. "Now we're going to plant beans, squash, chile, and corn in the garden. What's all this broccoli and brussel sprouts? They won't grow here, right?" That's

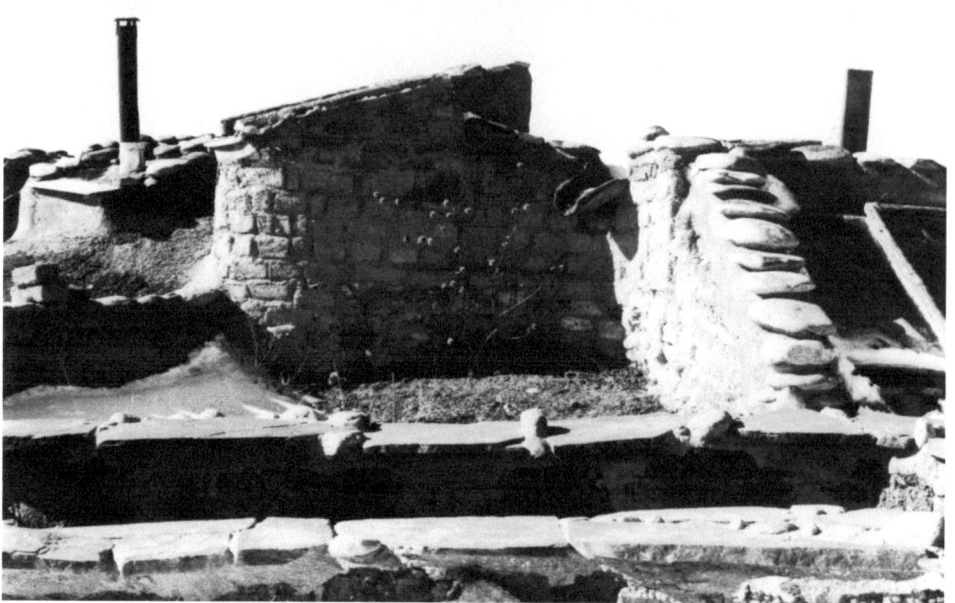

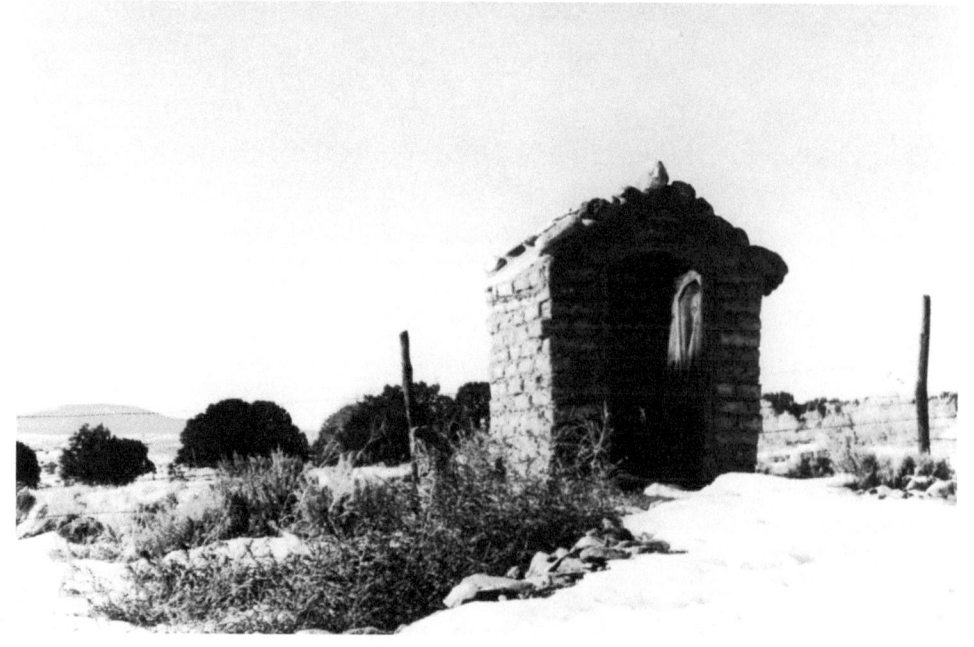

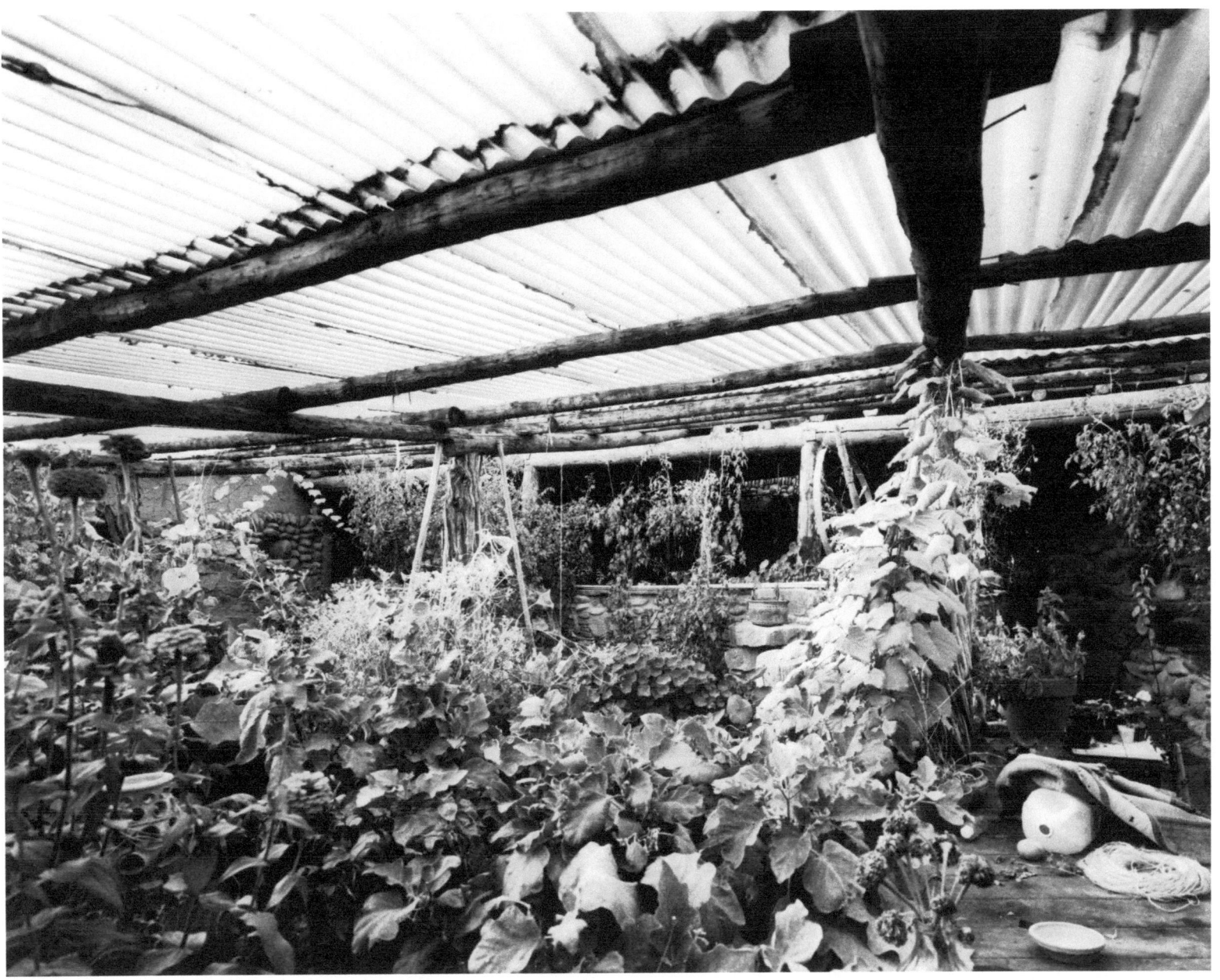

me. By the time the walls were up, I said, "It's huge. Just give me a little L-shaped traditional adobe house." Some part of me was outraged at this house for a long time—it overwhelmed me. Now I find it's friendly and joyful living here.

I'm still coming to terms with its openness. I tend to want to close off and have a private place. But this forced me to open up as a person far more than I would have otherwise.

We've worked up to this experience on many levels. We remodelled several houses before we built this one. Then our kids didn't fit regular schools, so we started our own. It's as if we're not satisfied with what is, so we push out into what we don't even know.

The whole house is so symbolic. There's the dungeon down below, the cave, the bowels, just like a person. Every spring water creeps into the root cellar and storage room because the back-hoe dug into the water table. Now we're working out a system with pipes and valves to control the water and use it.

The roof was really something—it just grew together. Every time ten or more people were here, we'd get up another beam. It's hard to imagine how simple it once was.

My 17-year-old daughter says, "Mom, I'm going to make me a house and it's going to be a two-room, square adobe house with windows all around." That's the way it has to go; the kids will do it another way.

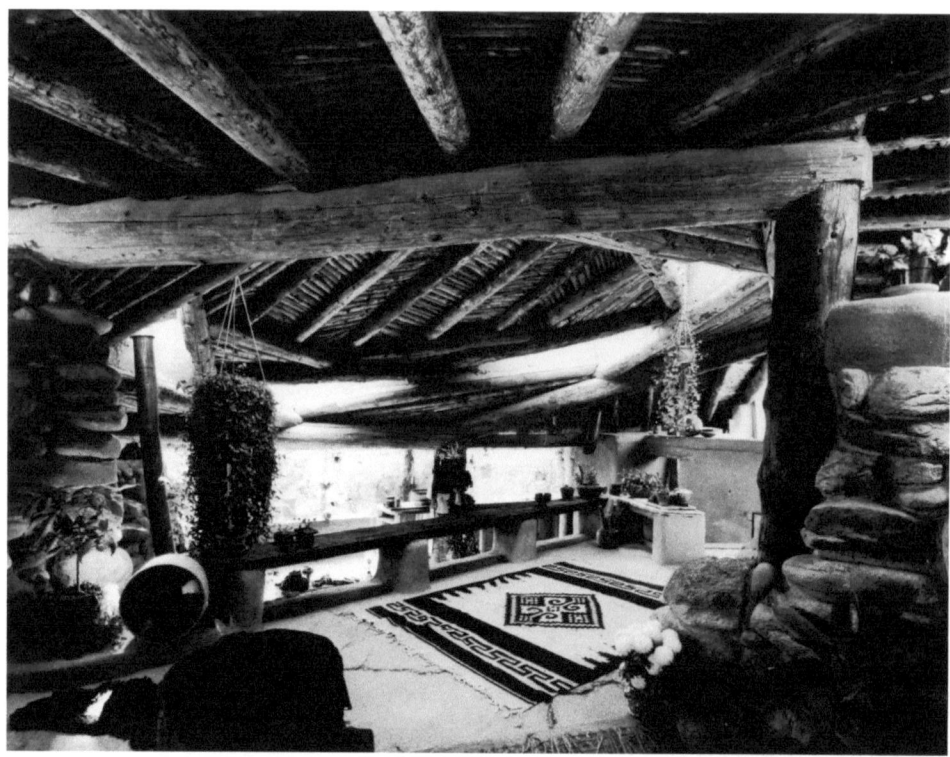

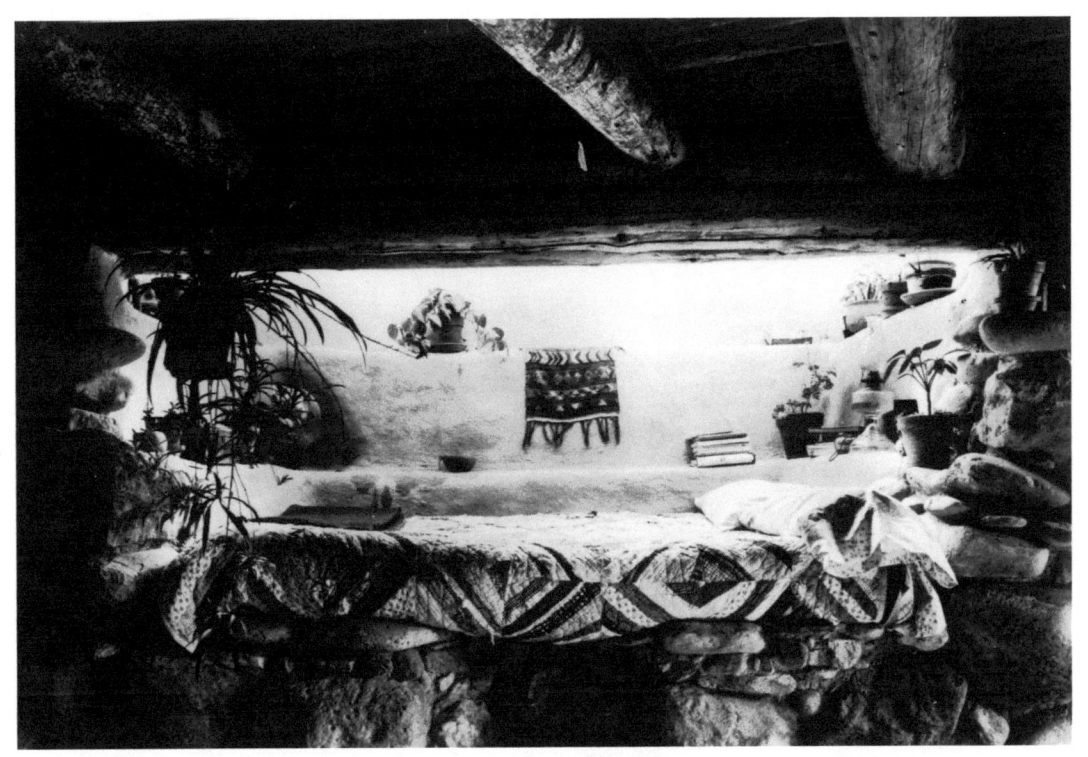

What a momentous undertaking. I mean if we knew ahead what we were getting into, we probably wouldn't have dared. Innocence, or lack of self-consciousness, is one of the mysterious gifts life gives. We just go ahead with what courage we have and do it anyway.

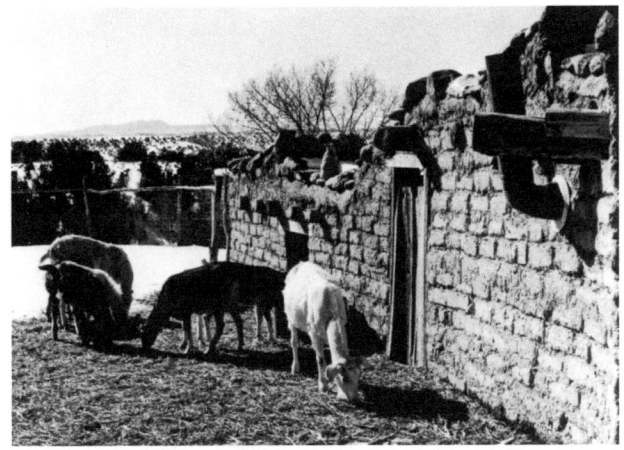

CASTLE & GOAT PENS

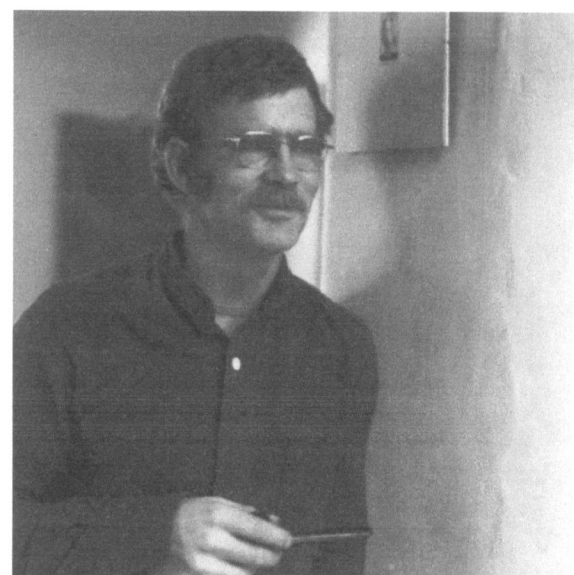

CHARLIE RAMSBURG, *painter, bought a house in the country—a partially built shell.*

CHARLIE: It was weird. I came back from Italy and was on my way to California and stopped here to visit a friend. After a while I ran into another old friend, then a long lost cousin on the plaza. I decided to stay on and began looking for somewhere to live. I saw several houses I didn't like and then a place in the country, a truly beautiful old scene with trees all around, but no roof. Just adobe walls and goat pens outside. Never having done any building—I didn't even know how to pronounce *viga*—it seemed a bit much.

Then I came here, wandered around and and felt at least there was something to relate to. A house was essentially here. Sitting in the swing in the cottonwood tree I said why not, and bought it. My whole life changed.

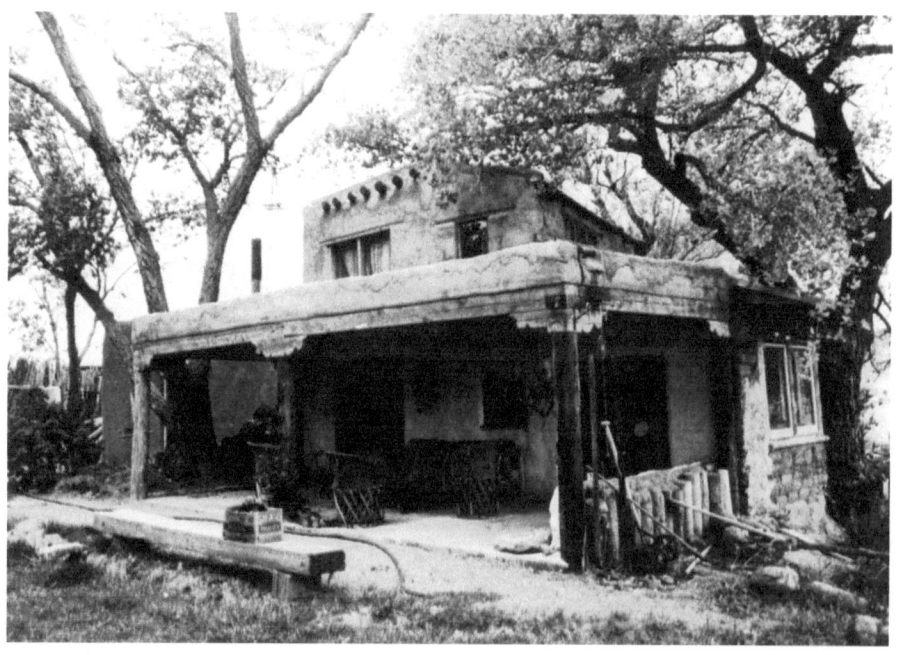

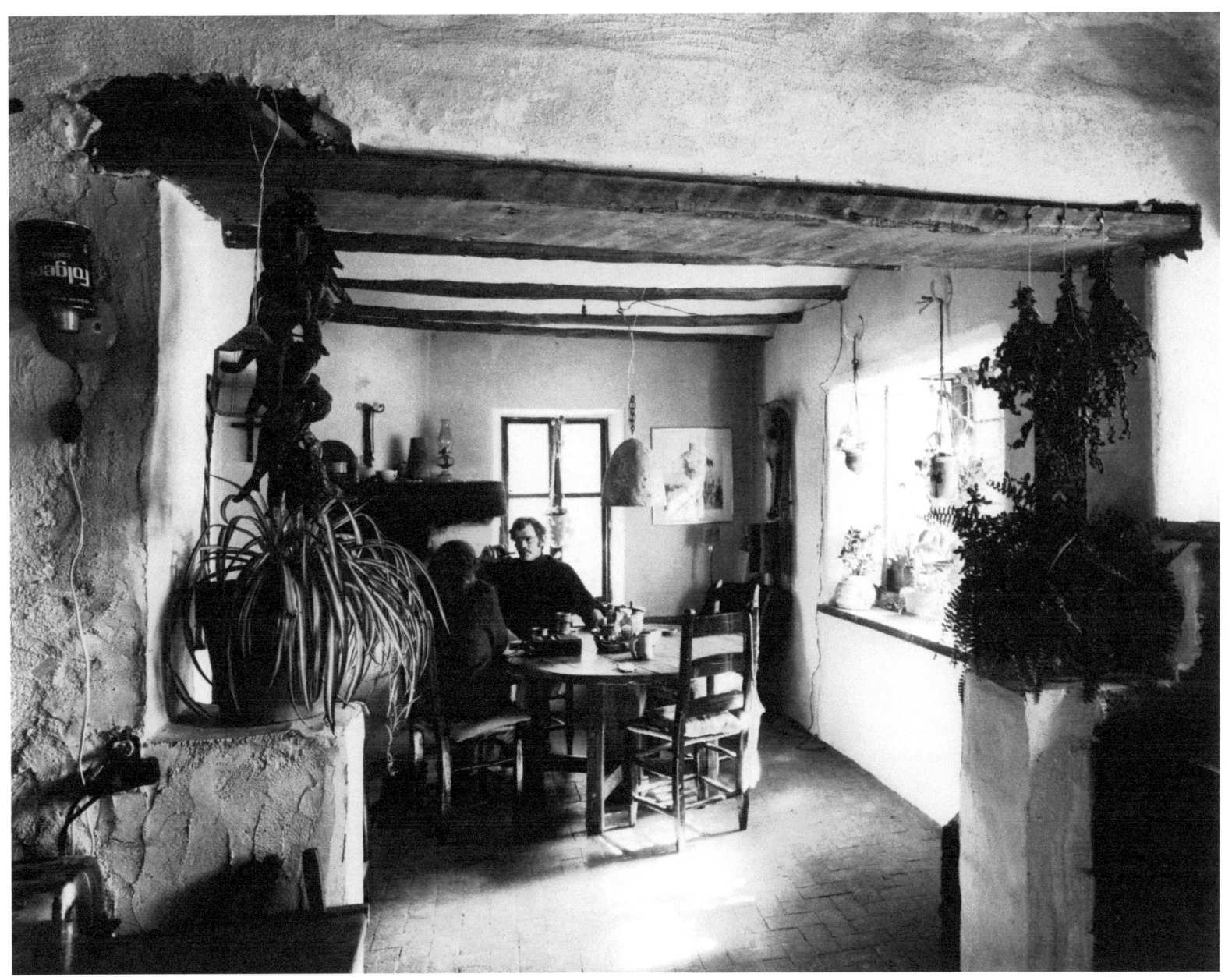

I needed time. I'd been running away, looking for answers all over the world, and finally said, forget it, I'll stay here three years and see what happens. That was 1971. I had nothing else to do then so I moved in and started working—all day and into the night.

That first winter I lived in one room. The other rooms were caving in—no windows, no doors, no plumbing. It was marvelous, camping out in this huge castle. I didn't really know what I had—with snowdrifts in the living room and the space so full of junk.

First, I got the kitchen working, the water running, then the icebox. Next I made the bedroom liveable. It's been a process of going around the house, fixing this room a bit, enlarging the next, then going back and editing, taking out stuff and doing it *right*.

When I first moved in, the hallway was completely different. I tried a partition and cabinets, and then tore out everything. That changed the whole flow of the house. I sat down and just looked at it until I decided what to do. I added a porch outside and made an entranceway like the spout of a bottle. You shoot through a narrow space and burst into the house.

I feel it's important to have the inside connecting to the outside, like windows across the end of the living room. That was a problem because I didn't want to go out the windows visually and get lost—either hung up in a lot of branches or tumbling over the dikes and into the guy's garage across the

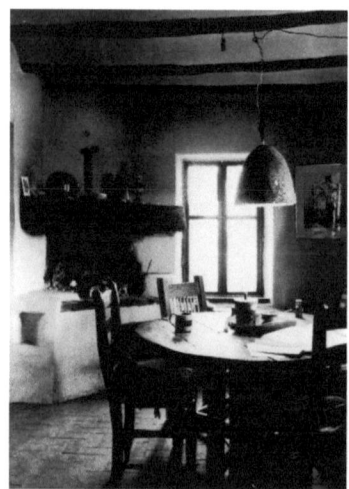

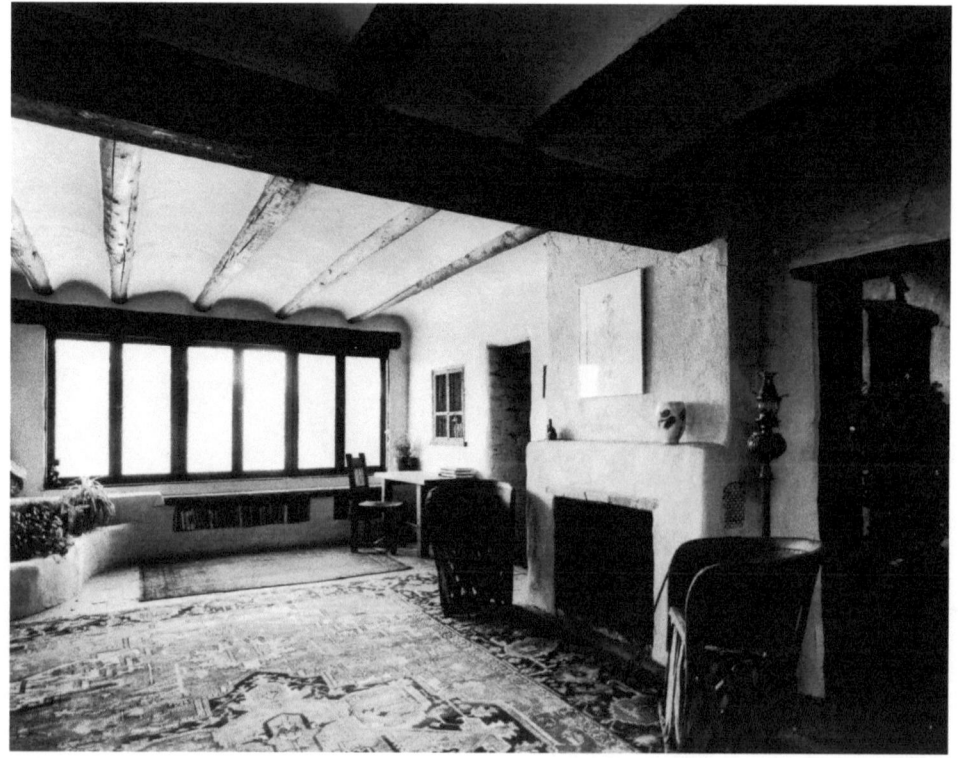

valley. So I expanded the windows and that brings the big tree up to the same plane and pops you back inside.

The first house you build you find out about yourself—the kind of space you need. Some people blow it because they design a house that seems idyllic to a certain fantasy, but has little to do with the reality of their life. Some spaces here are useless for my bachelor lifestyle; more space than I need seems an indulgence. Yet the living room has been fantastic. I don't really use it alone, but all kinds of strange events happen because I have that space—t'ai chi ch'uan, rehearsed plays, big dinner parties, weddings, all kinds of things. The room keeps changing to meet whatever situation arises; it's like the moveable part of the house.

Some houses are so personal they don't work for anyone else. Walking into a very subjective house can be a disadvantage. I prefer living here because it seems more universal and made for human beings. It's not like some houses that are so organic and gooey and intestinal, all esthetics, but unrelated to people.

It can be an addiction, this adobe building. A lot of people building houses are always looking for the perfect space, trying to find peace of mind through building. In my experience it was important during a certain period of my life, but I don't want to spend the rest of my life building adobe houses. There's so much else that needs doing.

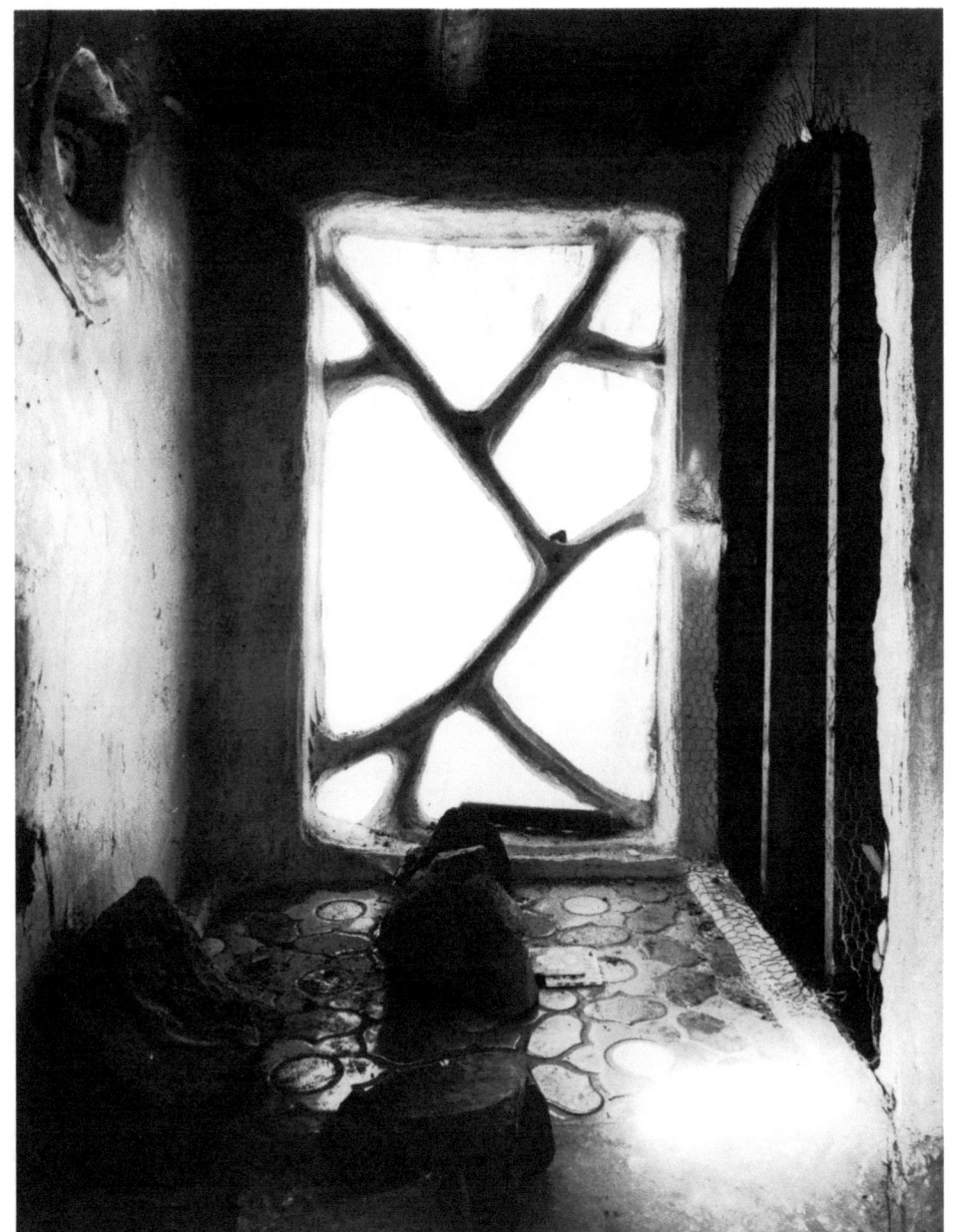

RACHEL BROWN *has lived in northern New Mexico for many years. Now that her children are grown she's writing a book based on her work as a weaver. She helped build the house she raised her family in and this earlier experience influenced her ideas about building. She began this house in 1974.*

RACHEL: I feel a house should be compact. My daughter was the first who lived with me here, and I thought of it as our own super little motel room. It has everything you need, but all very small.

At first it was just going to be a little room with no plumbing, but to satisfy the building inspector I had to add a bathroom and make the ceilings a certain height. It became a real project. I hired a crew of four or five guys more or less committed to twenty-five hours a week. A casual crew, but I wasn't paying them much so I can't complain and they did well. But I had to be on the job all the time, supervising every bit of it, and I hauled all the materials.

The house has steeply pitched roofs with a small room upstairs under the eaves.

I had my writing upstairs with a mattress in the corner. It was so cramped I decided to add a study off the main room. I asked my Spanish friend up the road if he could work it in. He showed up the next morning at 7:30 and three weeks later it was done. We figured the materials and had the lumber com-

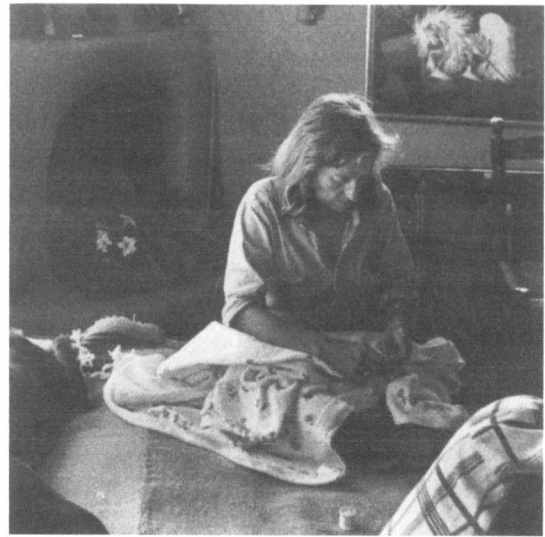

MUD & SYMMETRY

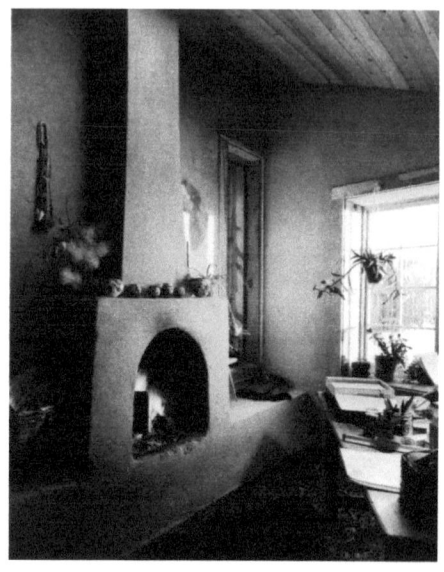

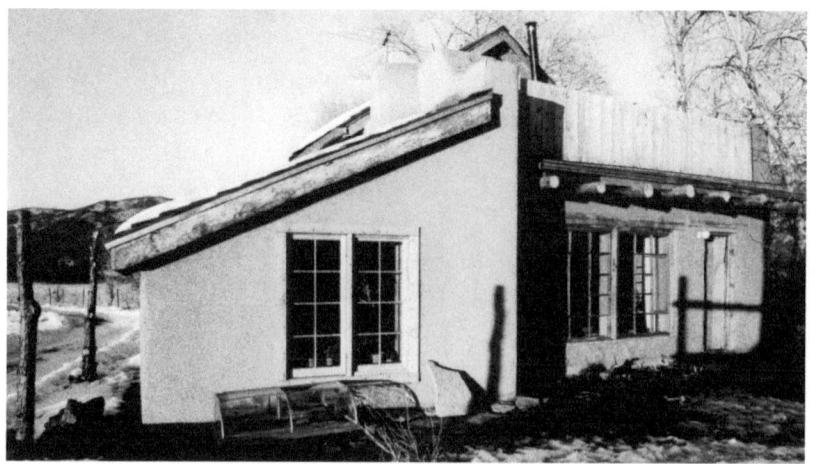

pany deliver them. Then he and his two sons just zoomed. It was incredible, a great way to build, and no more expensive, though I was paying him more than the first crew. He had all the tools, his own workshop and took great pride in his work.

The house is mostly heated by a wood stove in the downstairs living space. The stove pipe gives heat as it goes up through the bedroom.

A couple of loads of wood is enough for the winter. Heating is one of the biggest problems around here and it's amazing people don't consider it more when building. This house is really together being small and easy to heat. I prefer small rooms because in the summer you can move outdoors, and in the winter I hate being cold.

A lot of houses are inefficient, with gangly rooms, nooks and crannies and extensions which don't mean anything. Too many are trying to be asymmetrical just for the sake of being different and turn out to be rather uncomfortable. I love symmetry and the only reason this house isn't symmetrical is this piece of land wouldn't allow it.

Now I'm going to build another little house, just a bit bigger. It's going to be very traditional: a two story adobe with a pitched cedar roof and dormer windows, a central entrance hall with a kitchen on one side and a living room on the other, stairway to two upper bedrooms side by side. Then after that I'm planning "super house."

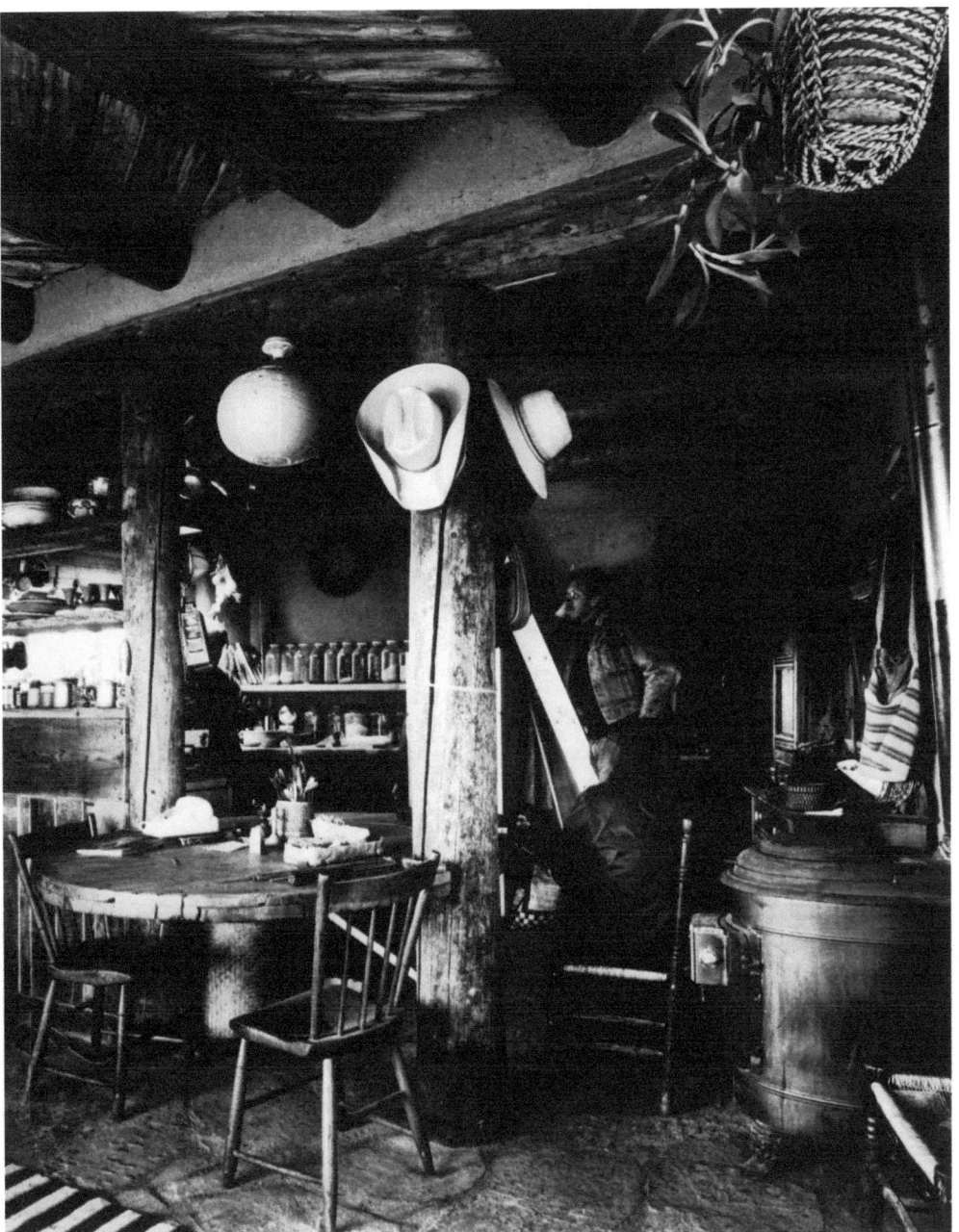

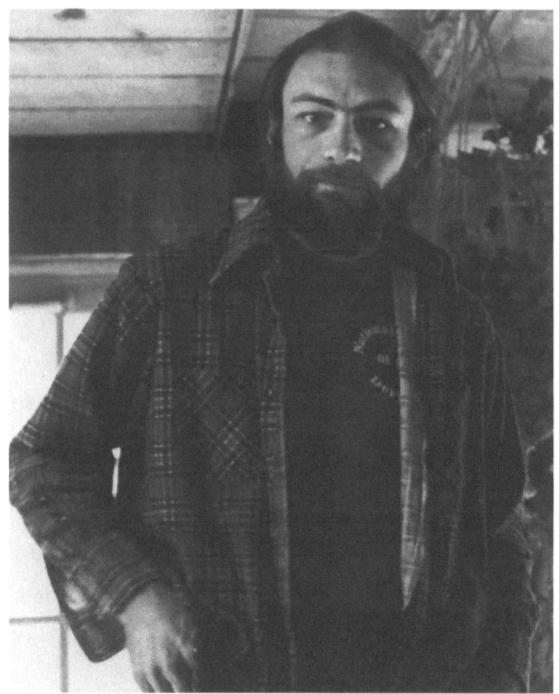

MOUNTAIN WATCHER

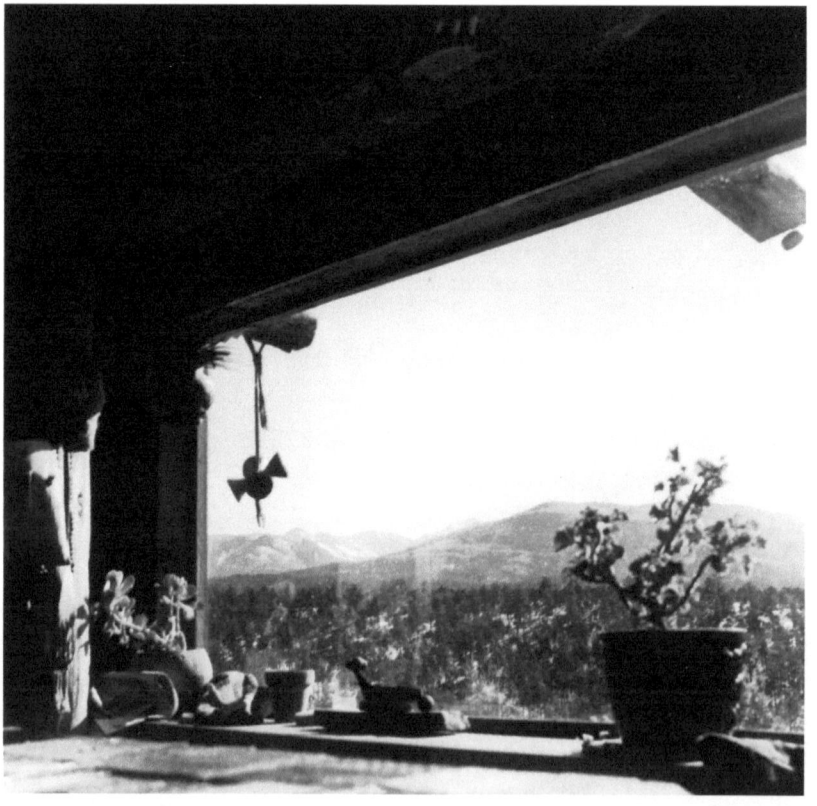

Reno's studio

A.K.A. RENO'S *house is on the edge of a high plain overlooking a valley in the Sangre de Cristo Mountains. The original house was typical of traditional Spanish-American building with several rooms in a row, no hallway, viga ceilings and a steeply pitched tin roof to shed the snow.*

RENO: Why do I like living here? See that big mountain over there—I like it. And it's so quiet here.

The house was built in the early thirties. This was a community of two hundred people then. The house served as a home, then as a dance hall. When I bought it in 1969 it had been vacant for twenty years. Only the shell was still standing. Stuff was lying around and

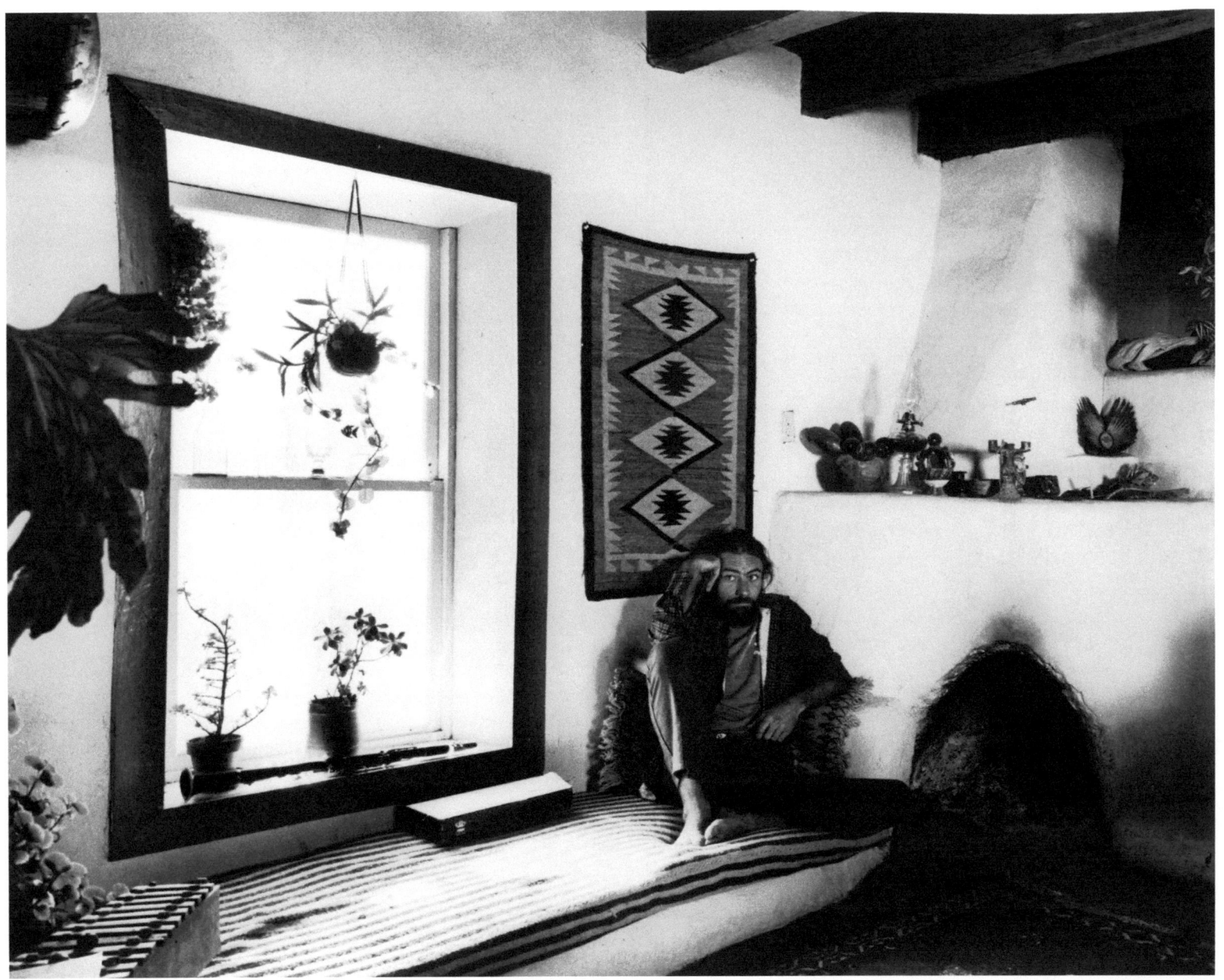

inside were shoulder high mounds of dirt. You could see four layers of wallpaper. The interior adobe walls were wobbly so I reinforced them and made them solid. I saved as much of the original house as I could—the linear arrangement of rooms and the windows. For the first three years we lived without power. Mushrooms grew in the living room as there was seepage from melting snow. When we moved in there were no fireplaces and now we have two.

It was dark in here for a long time, so we put in a window to the south. That turned into a doorway opening onto the dining room we eventually added. Later I extended an end wall of the dining room and made a greenhouse along the south side. Heat from the greenhouse spreads through the house by day and the flagstone floor, being heat absorbent, gives off warmth at night.

For the first couple of years all the materials were scrounged. I used wood I found around here and tore down an old adobe and salvaged the bricks. Finally, we had more money and did most of the major remodelling. We also built my woodworking shop and a guest house next door. One of the hardest things to figure was how to tie the two buildings together esthetically. We built a portal along the north side of the old house and another around the new one. That did it.

My father was an architect, so I've been around building although I never did any myself before. I just charged into it and my head's still jumping with ideas.

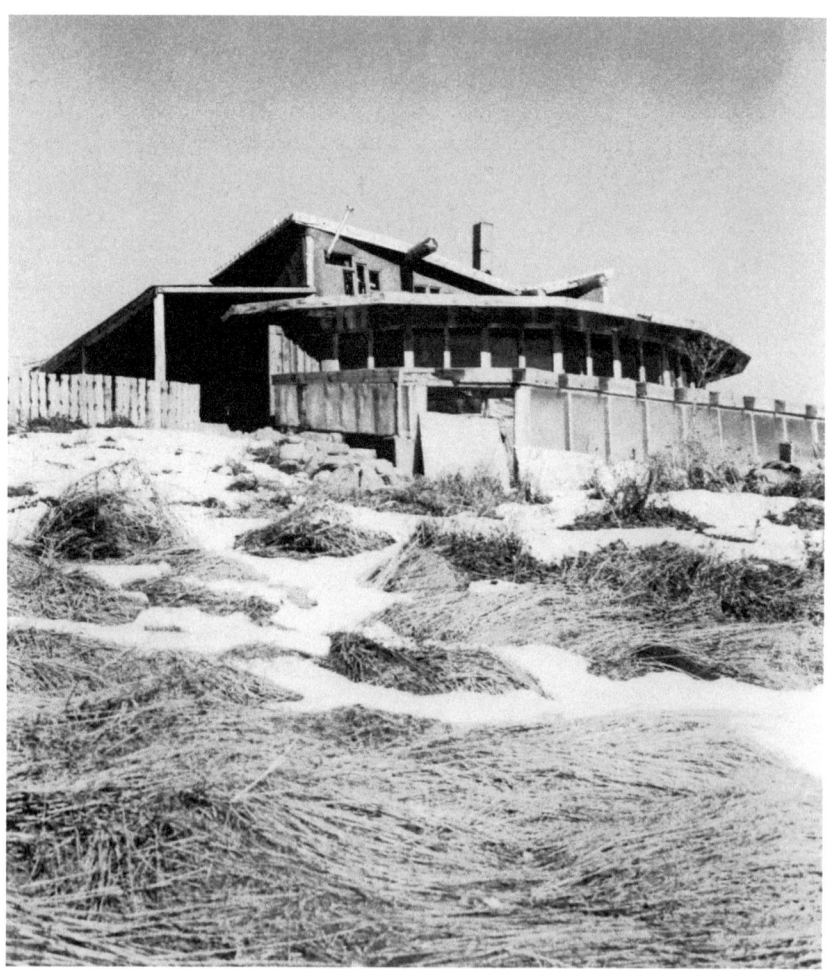

Reno's studio

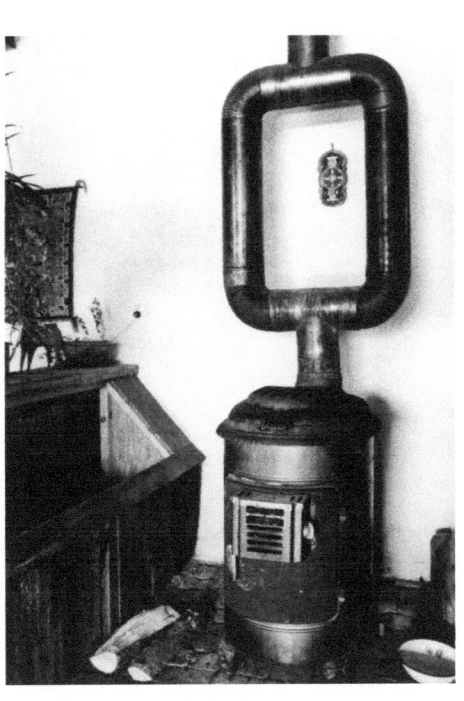
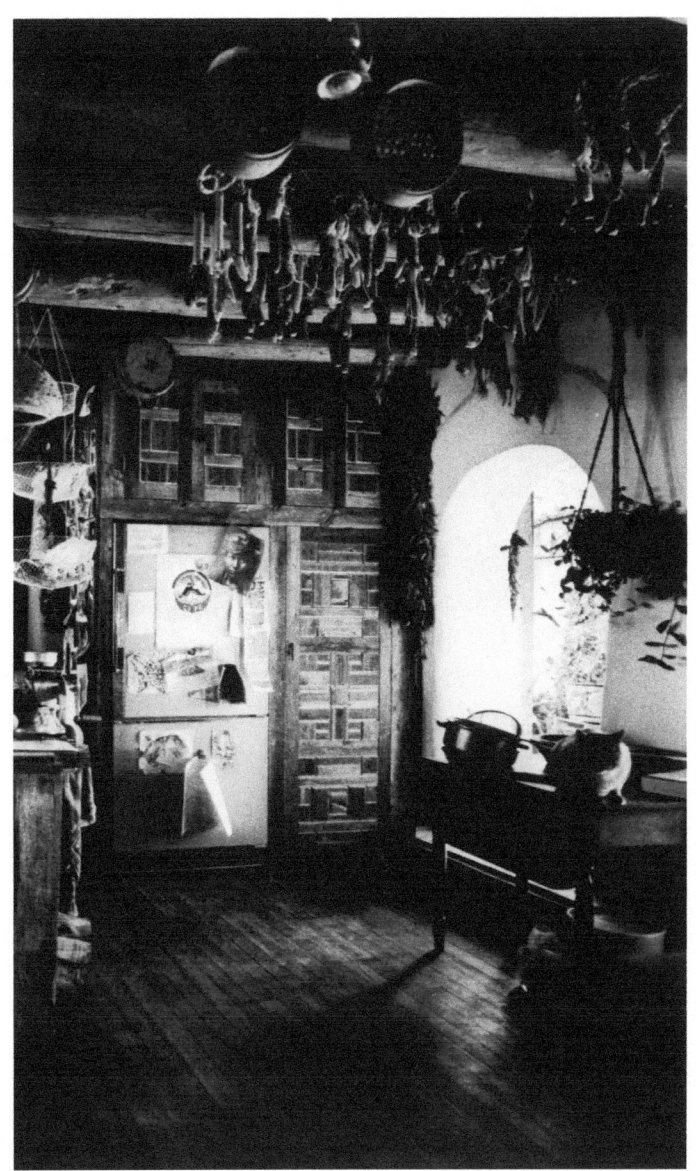

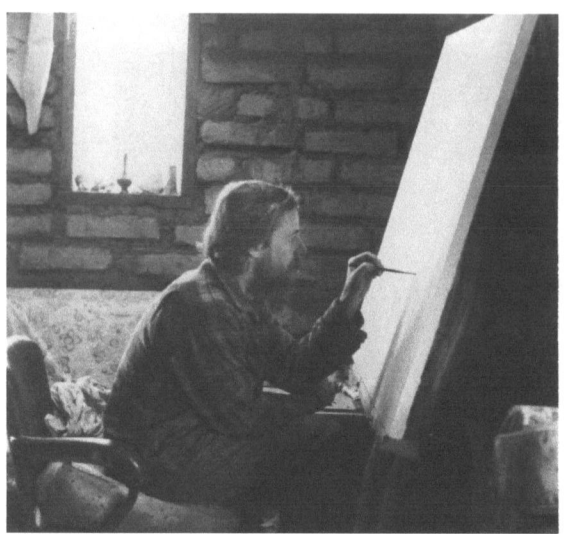

ROUND HOUSE

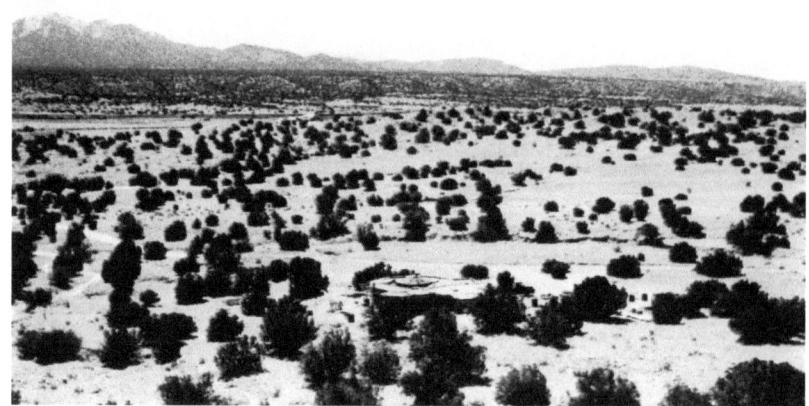

DENNIS CULVER, *painter and rock musician, built the house he and* NANCY *live in over a period of two years. He had no previous building experience and started a summer house just to see what he could do. Then, as he says, it got more involved. Two rooms were added to the original circular space and now they live here all year long.*

DENNIS: I scratched a circle on the ground, then a friend came with his tractor and we went around and around and dug part of it back into the hill. That left a big scar sitting here. I didn't have materials or know anything about building, but another friend dropped by who'd just finished pouring foundations for a house, and he said, "Let's get it on." In two days we poured the footings—about two feet deep and eighteen inches wide—right into the ground.

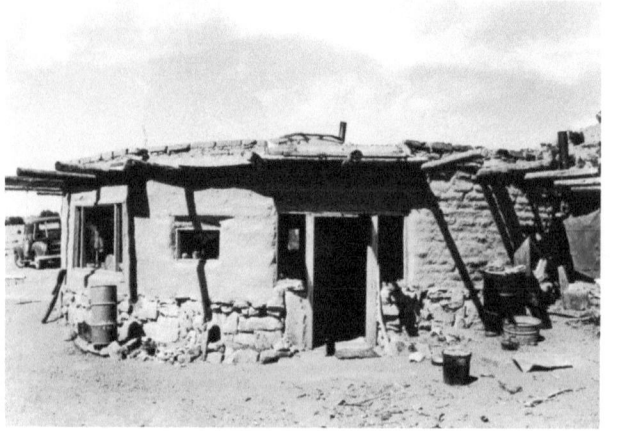

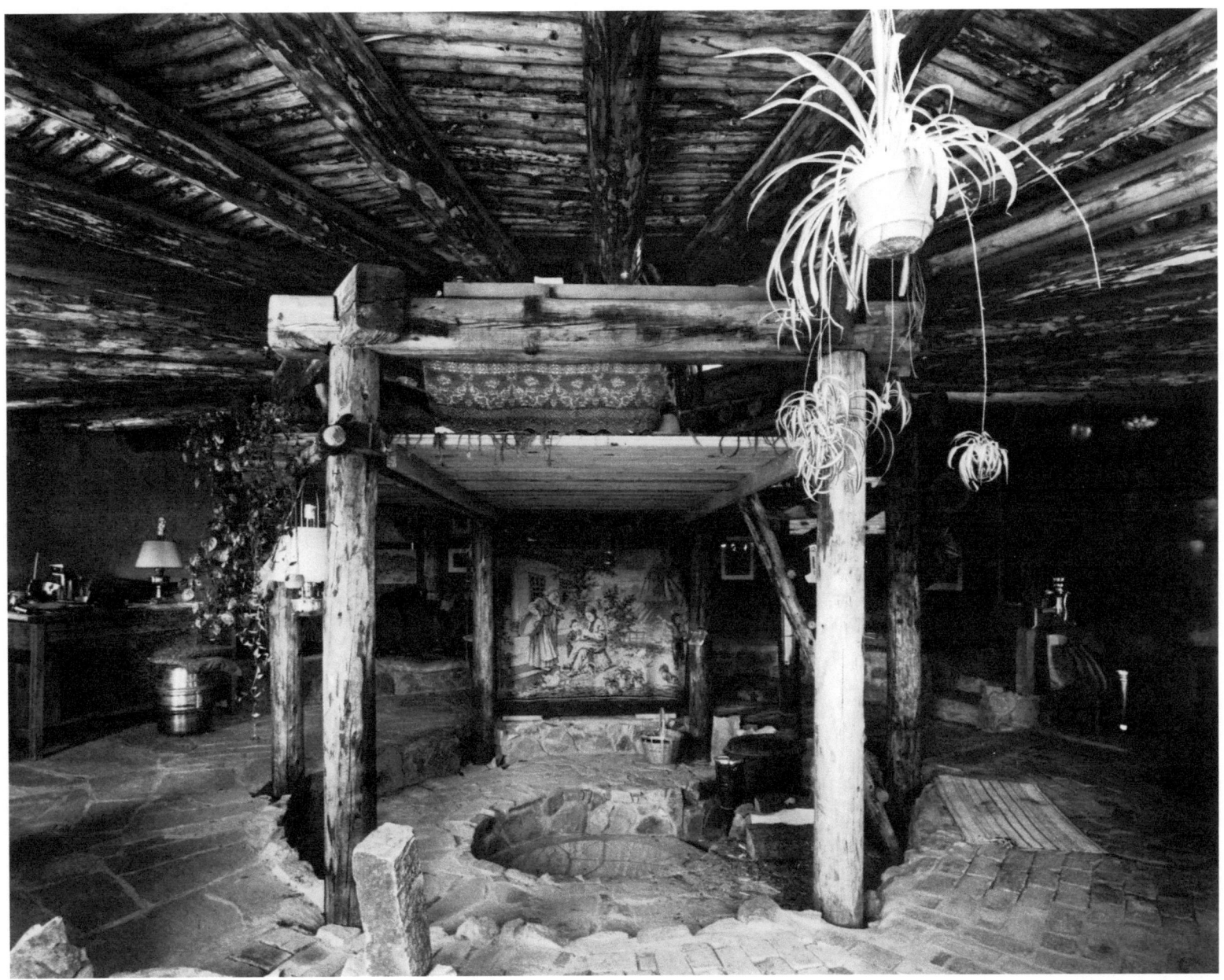

The rock foundations above the footings took a long time since I was working mostly alone. Once I started laying adobes it went faster. A friend taught me how to make the adobes and there's good soil here. I just had a long pile of dirt and I'd make a volcano or dish shape in it and pour in fifty-five gallons of water, some asphalt and straw. I shovelled the mud into wood forms to make bricks and let them cure in the sun. Because the stone foundations are high and the space is open, I needed only seven hundred bricks.

I started straining mud for the mortar, taking out all the rocks. The first course alone took me two days. Then it rained the next day. So this guy who builds fireplaces came by and said, "Hey, are you interested in getting those walls up?" We forgot about the rocks and dumped two hundred gallons of water into a pile of dirt and began making mortar. Soon people were crawling all over, coming around the walls handing me bricks. It really went up fast.

It took a while to figure out the center part with the stove and sleeping loft. If I'd paid more attention I would've pitched the roof all the way around and the loft could have gone higher. One reason it's so funky is because once I decided to live here full-time, certain immediate things had to get done. Without electricity or running water, I had to work fast with the materials on hand.

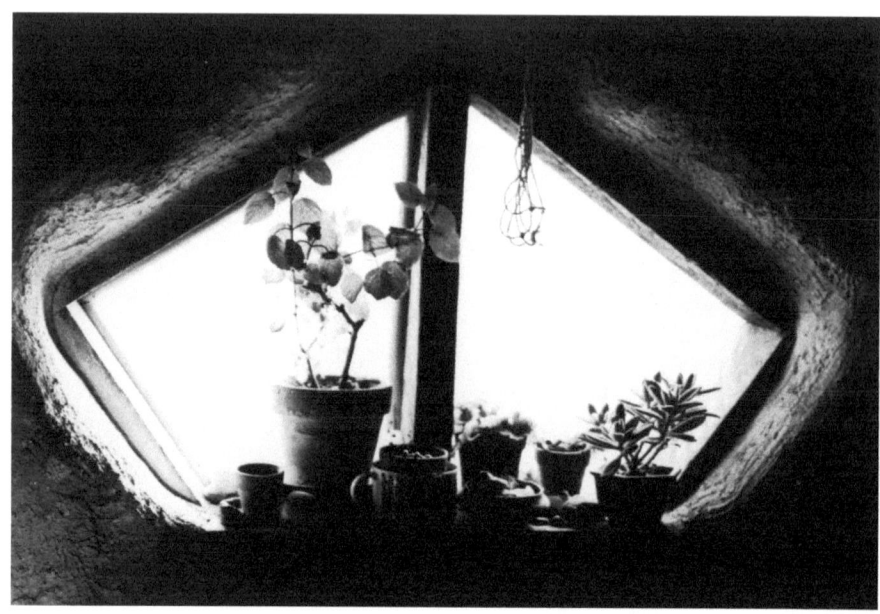

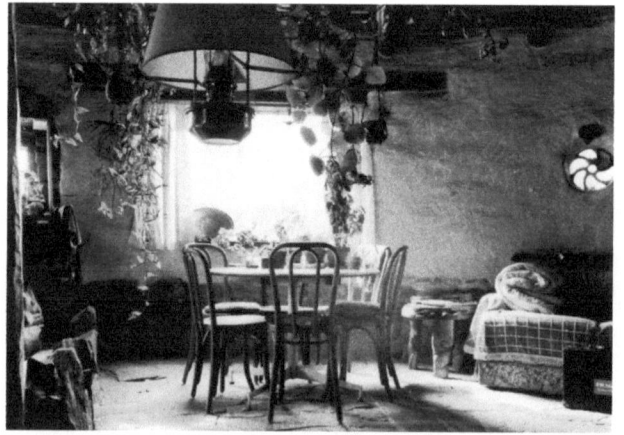

NANCY: It's not easy to find furniture to fit a circle; like square kitchen cabinets against a curved wall. That was weird for a while, but I like the space. People naturally gravitate around the stove, and it's practical for heating, being below floor level. I like a big, open kitchen. When we have people over I'm not cut off from the goings-on.

A round house gives a different flow of space than a square one—no corners for energy to get trapped in. The Indians say round space is the most spiritual and satisfying, but I never really understood that until I'd lived in a tipi.

Here I feel people come in, sometimes, with heavy energies and somehow, the round shape just takes that energy and disperses it. May be superstition on my part, but nothing bad has happened in all the time we've been here.

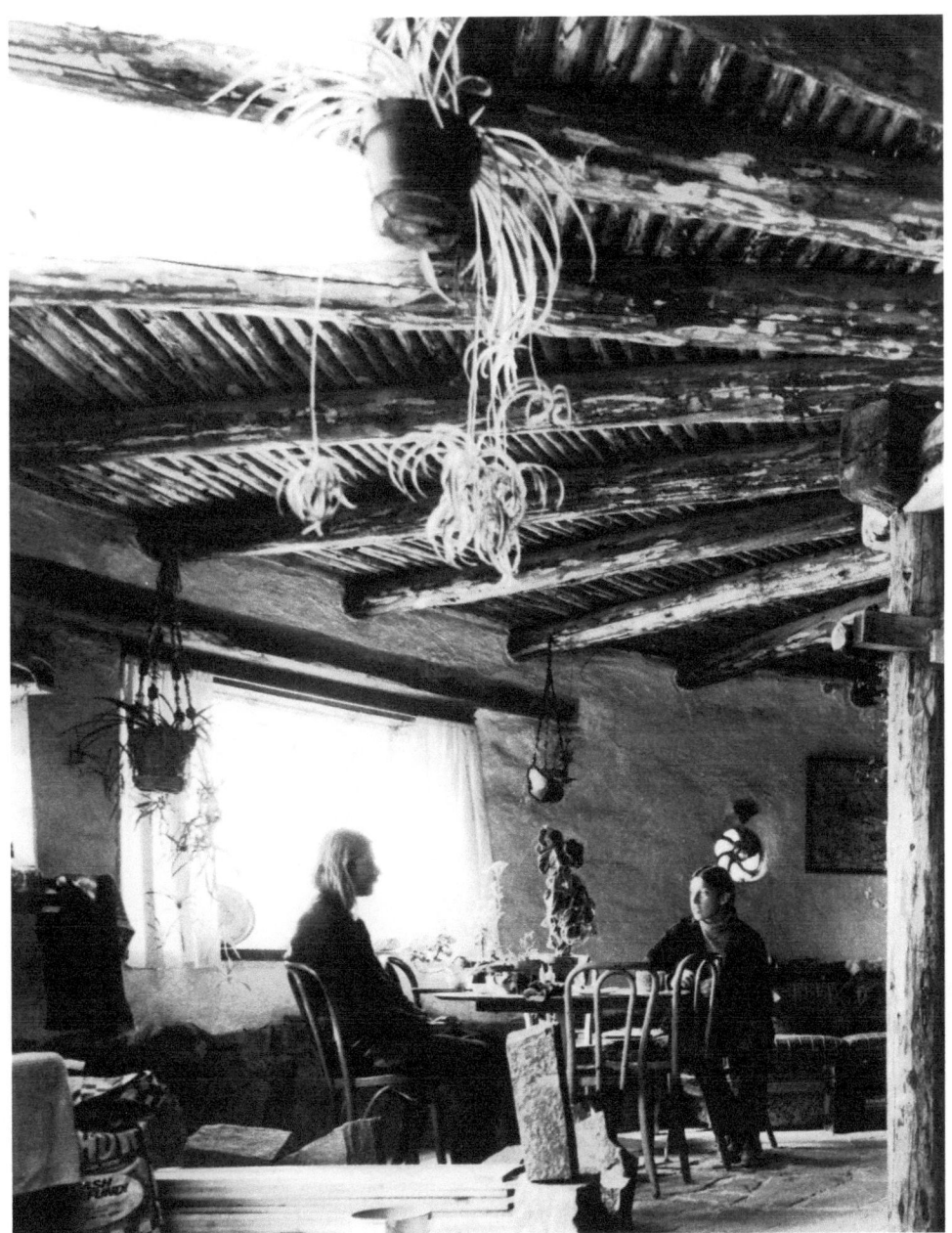

PIT HOUSE

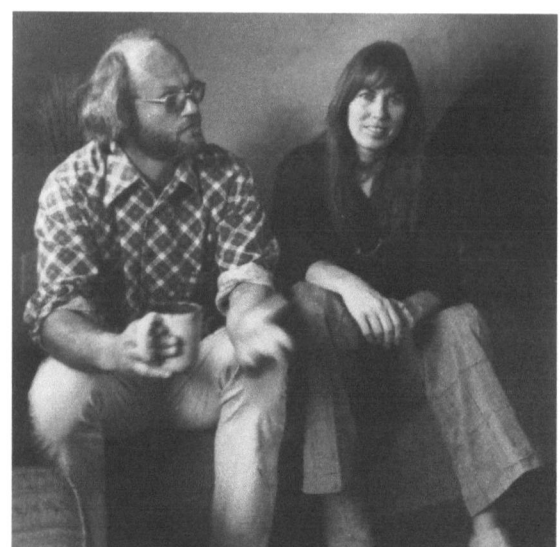

JOHN and GEORGIE MCGOWAN *lived in Colorado where he was the city engineer for a small town. Their present house is in a suburban area in New Mexico, but is entirely unlike its neighbors. Part of the house is underground and emerges from the earth.*

JOHN: I was driving down from Colorado and stopped at Mesa Verde to watch the excavation of an ancient pit house. I thought it would be nice to build something like that someday. Several years later, in 1974, we started this house. We didn't want to work from plans, but soon learned that building codes require them. I made a clay model of a pit house and then developed drawings. We projected the size of the house from the drawings and laid it out roughly on the land. From there we improvised. We couldn't work

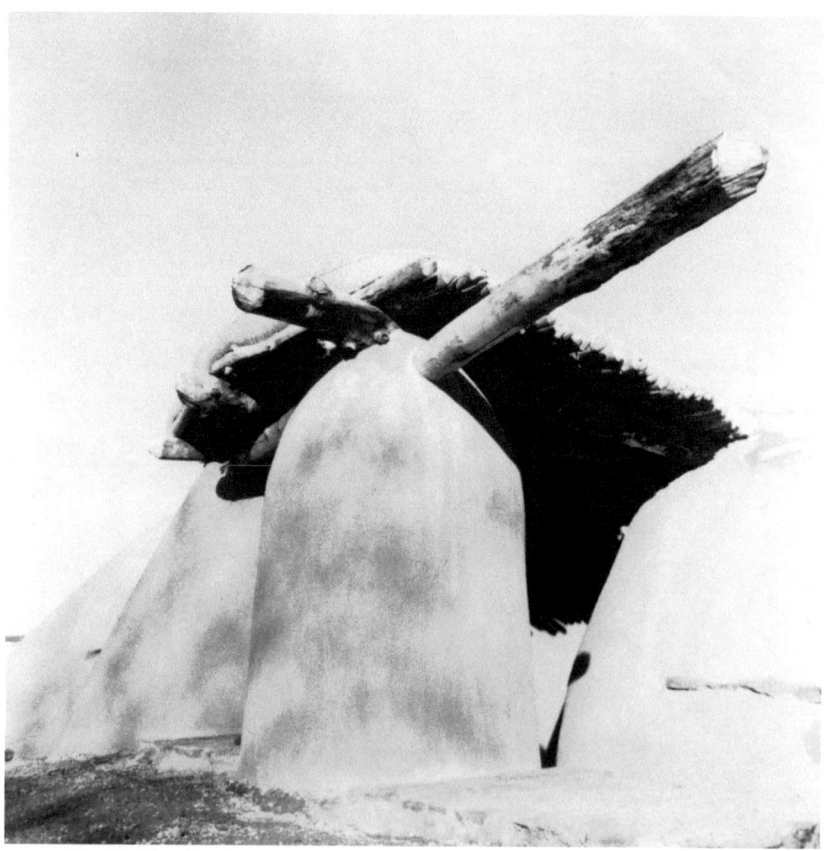

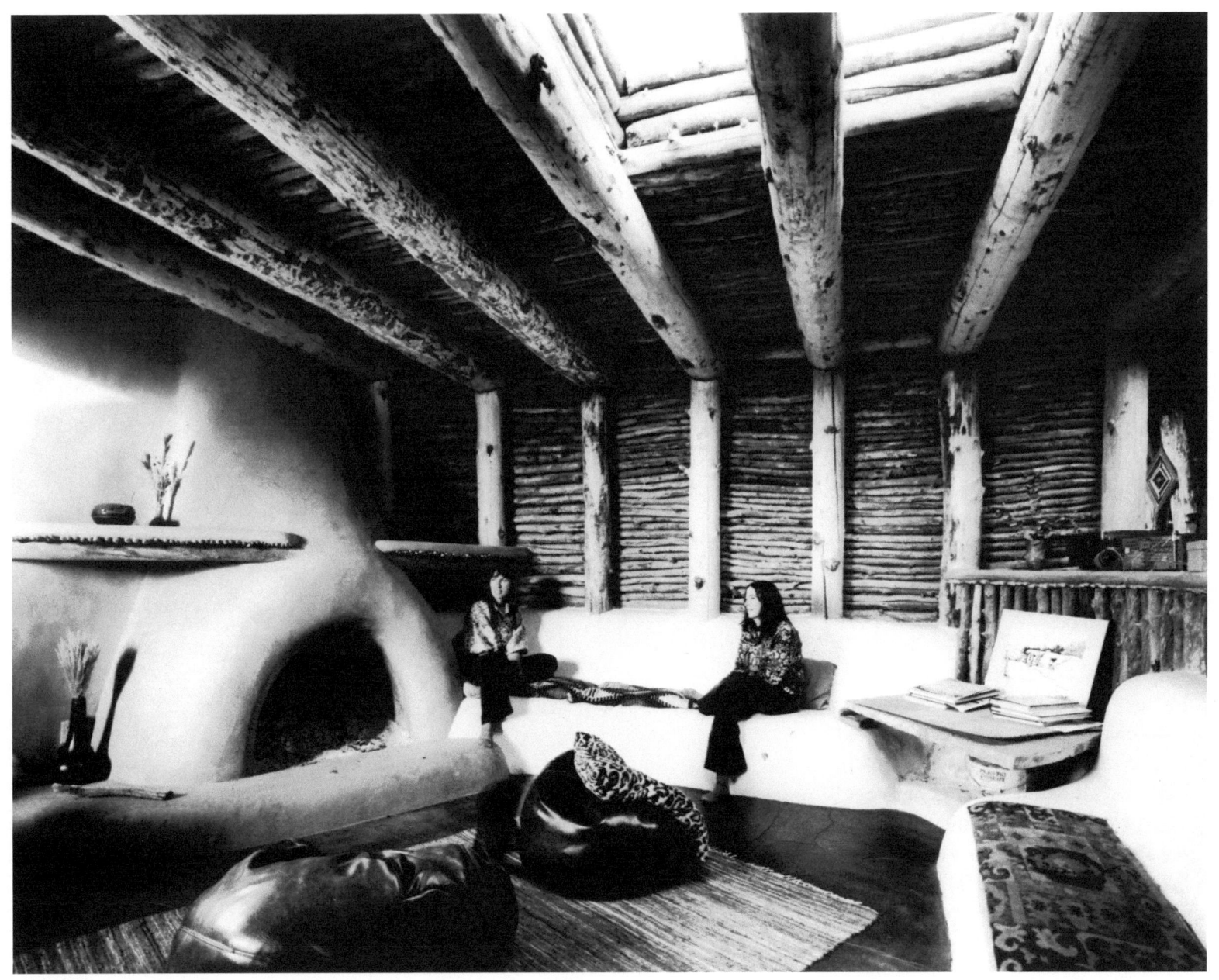

strictly by the plans because I could never see far enough ahead to achieve quite what I wanted. We didn't have a clear concept of where windows and skylights should be, so we worked those out as we went along.

We'd get to a certain stage and Georgie would say, "That doesn't look right—I think you can do better." That kept me from being so cock-sure of myself. The bathroom, for instance, worked out better because of what she conveyed.

The bathroom is built around an irregularly shaped bathing pool lined with brilliant turquoise blue tile. Plants spill from planters and hanging pots.

When the tub is full, it looks as though the house is built around a pool instead of a bath tub. We tried to keep the feeling of a natural hotspring and include the Japanese concept of washing in a shower before stepping into the pool.

Georgie and I wondered what it would be like, having guests in this nice pool. We were sitting by the fireplace with some friends, making idle conversation, and decided, well, let's take a dip. Georgie lit candles around the pool and we all eased in up to our shoulders. We only wondered why we'd wasted so much time sitting around when we could have been relaxing in the pool. Actually, the shape of the whole house encourages everybody to open up and relax.

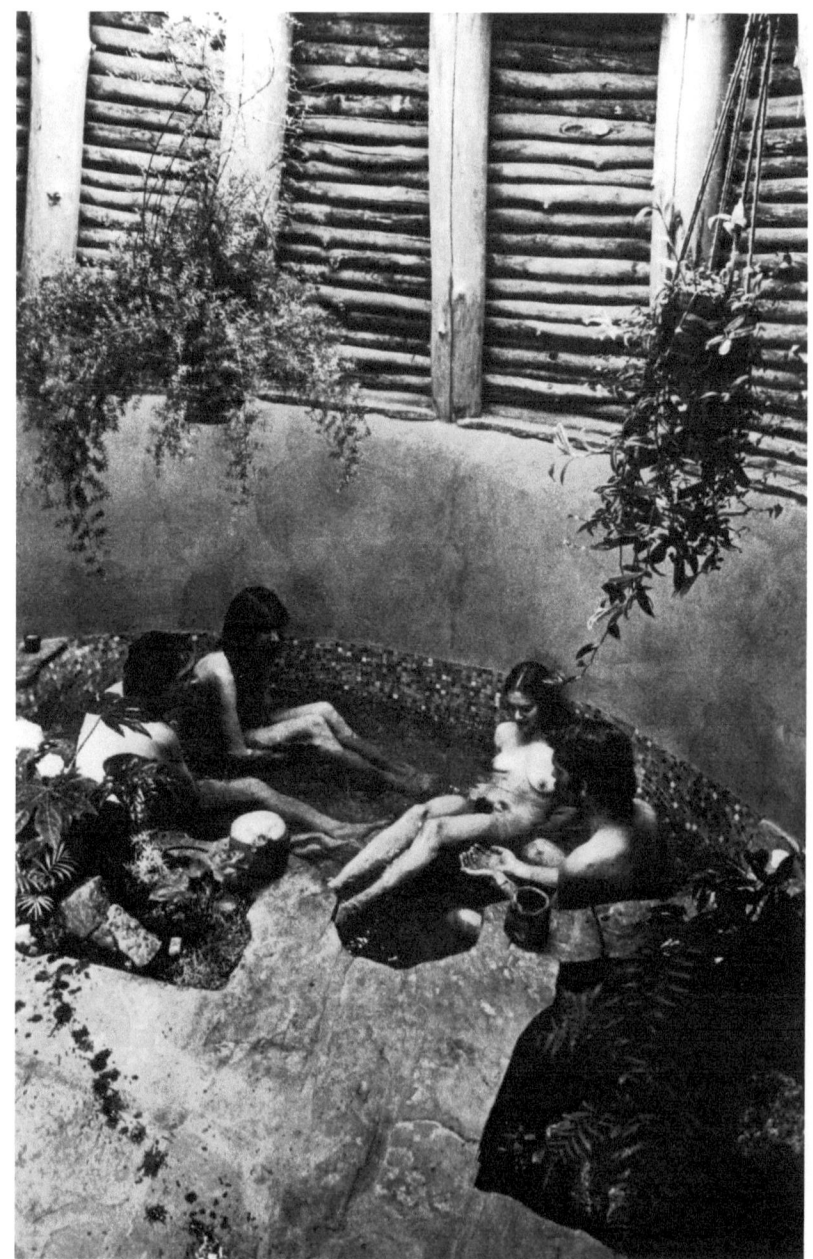

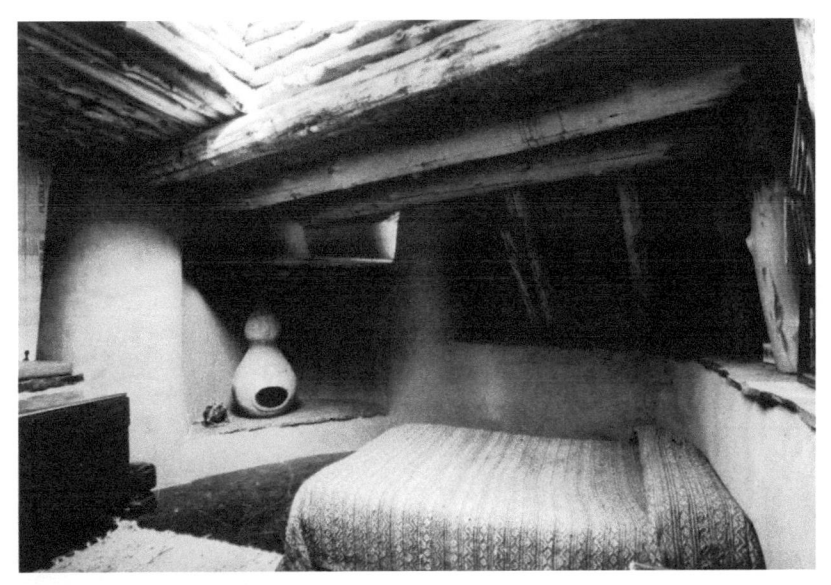
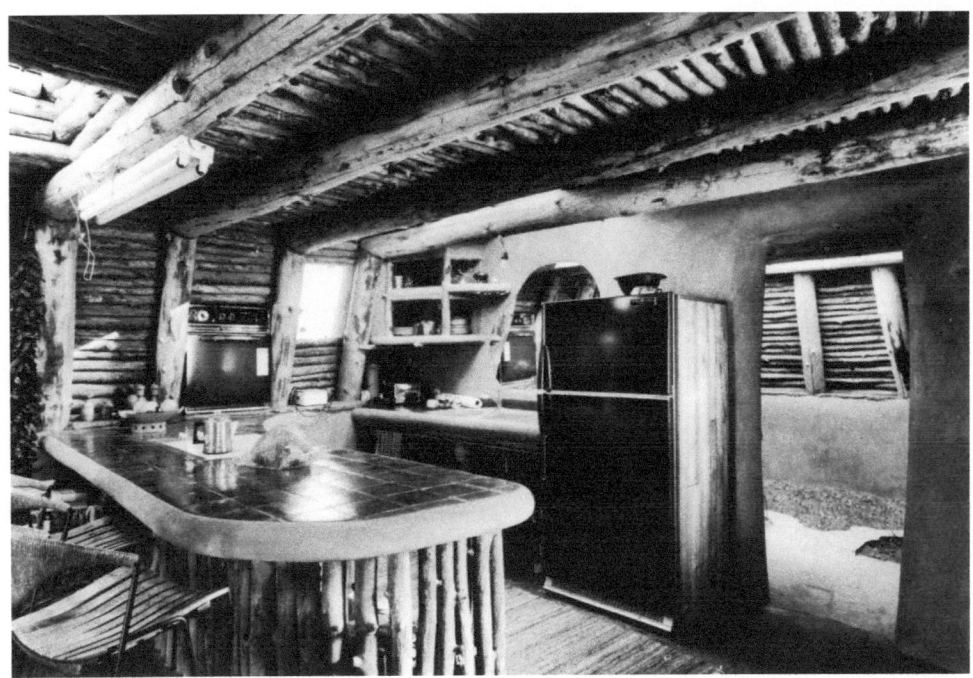

John's engineering experience is evident in the simple solidity of construction and in details, such as the fitting and hinging of the big windows. An efficient radiant heating system in the floor burns oil now, but soon will be switched over to solar power. The oil can still be used as backup fuel, if necessary.

JOHN: After you sit a while you get a picture of what the house is; kitchen and living room in one space, bathroom at the end, and where the bedroom is. No tricks, it's pretty straightforward.

GEORGIE: I visited Mesa Verde and saw the excavated pit house for the first time. Its shape was so familiar—just like our house. This kitchen is delightful; easy to work in and a joy to be able to see out.

The house accomodates regular furniture; cabinets, chairs and a bed, with more ease than we had expected. John wanted nothing in the house made of milled lumber, so we've used as little as possible.

JOHN: We gathered almost all the wood from the forest: pine vigas, aspen posts and latillas. They're free—all you need is a permit from the Forest Service.

This would be an expensive house to buy, but anyone can build a house like this without being wealthy. All you need is determination.

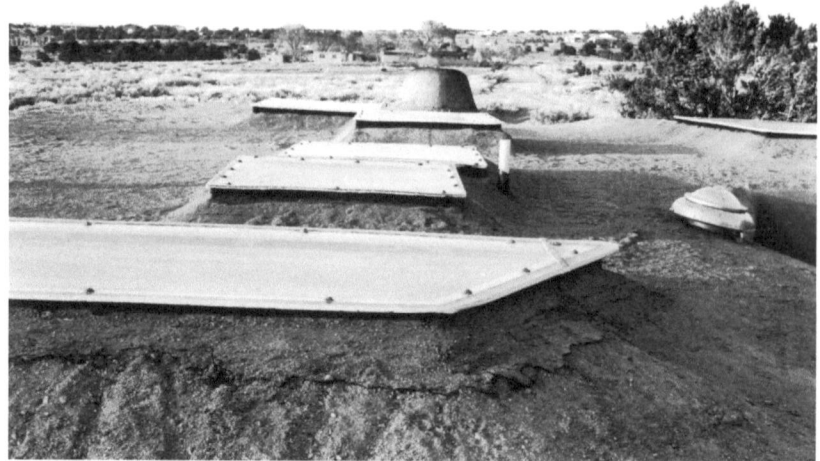

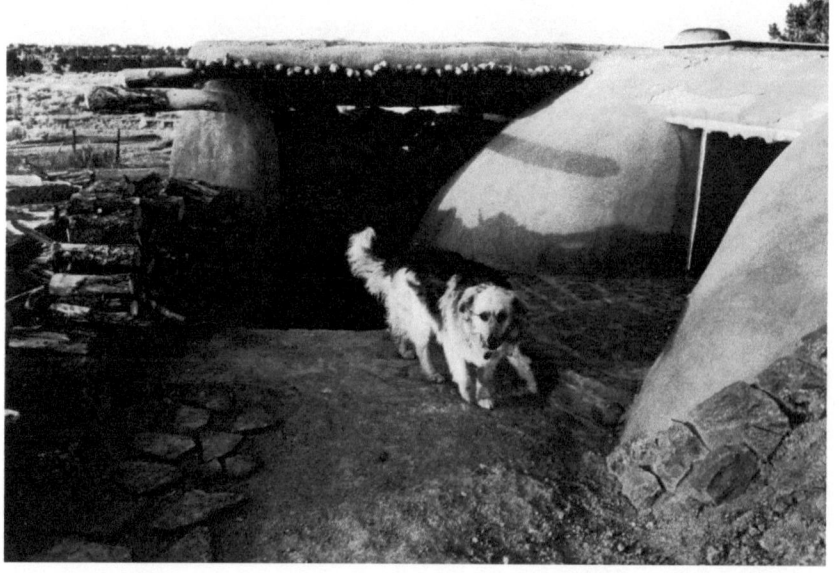

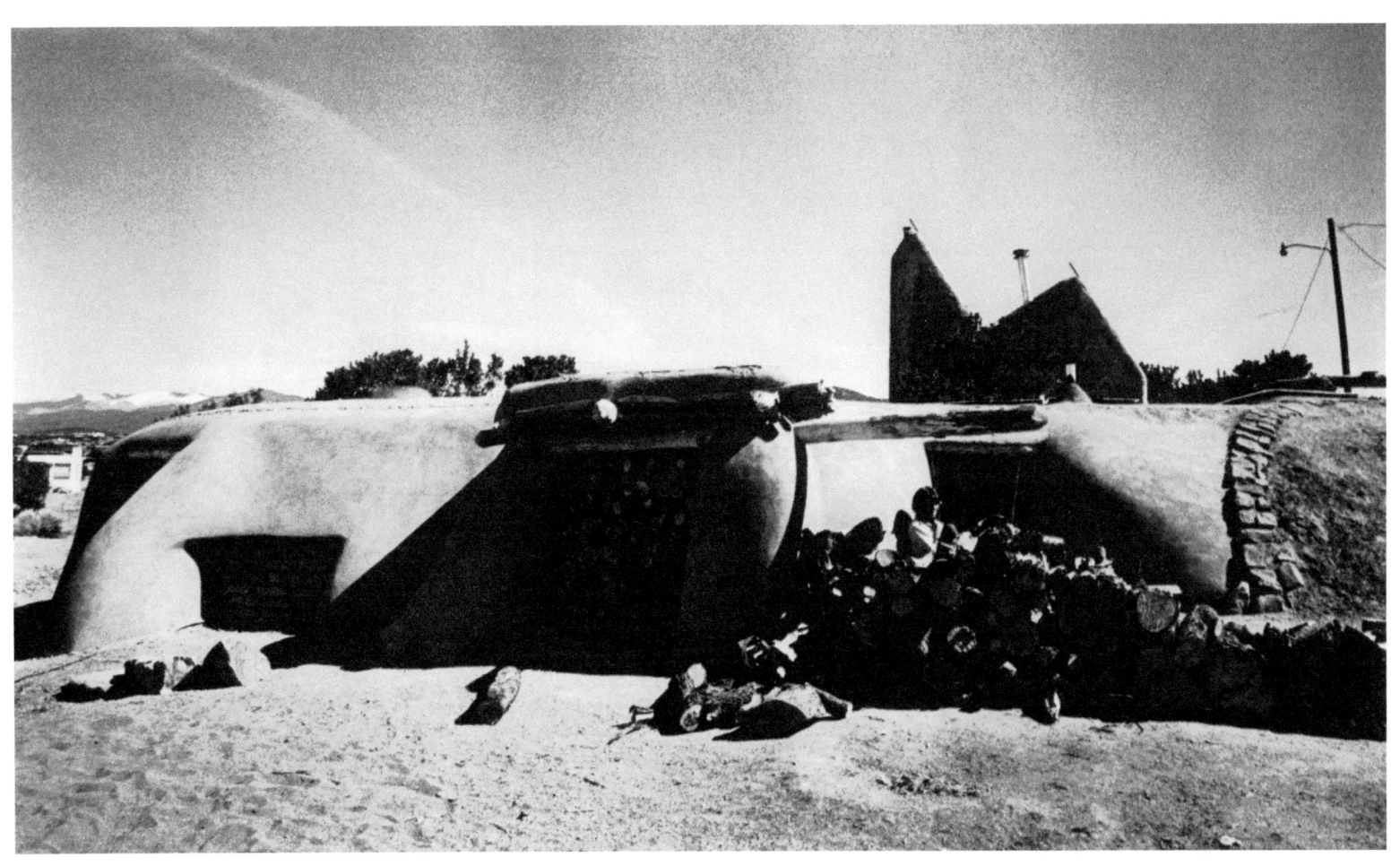

TREE ROOM

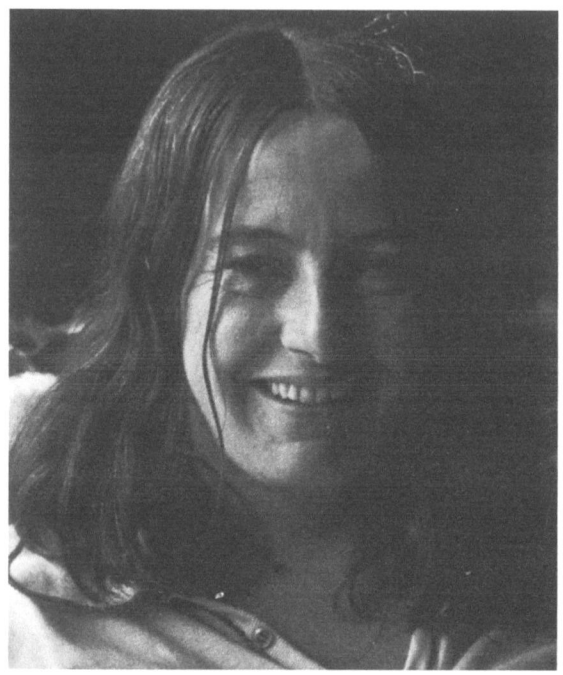

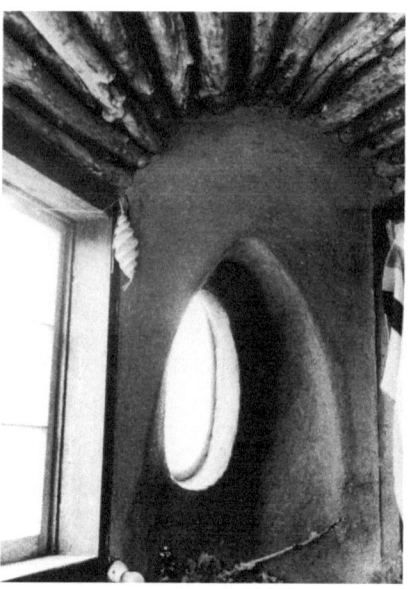

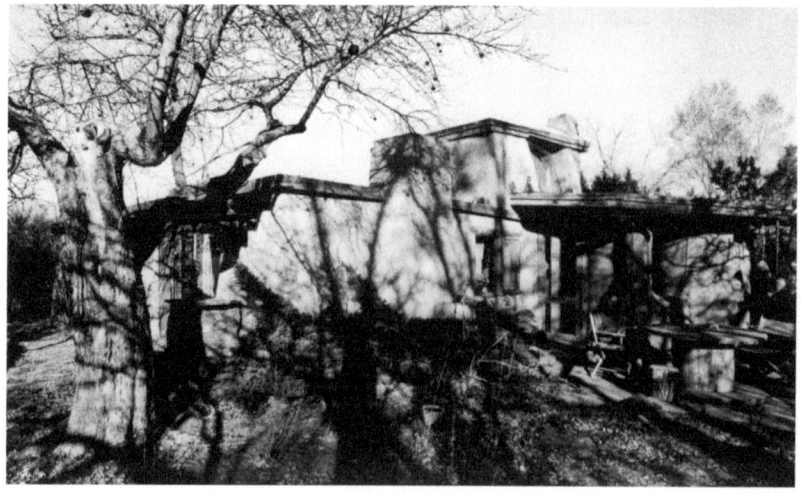

VIRGINIA GRAY *was raised in Cleveland and migrated to Santa Fe in 1953 where she lived in a converted chicken coop and apprenticed herself to a potter making wind bells. An architect friend encouraged her to build her own house and pottery workshop. He drew plans for the first section, a simple rectangle, and taught her to build a stone fireplace. She soon was up to her elbows in cement, and also put hammers, saws and wrenches to work.*

VIRGINIA: After living in a barn where potter's clay, pots and pans, and toothbrushes all shared the same sink, it was an incredible luxury to build a house with three sinks. At first the living space was ample, but over the years it became crowded. By 1970 I wanted not only more space, but also to break out of the rectangle. I wanted curving walls and space up high, an aerie. I made a number of fretful sketches, never satisfied with any of them, until I realized it was more important to get something done than seek perfection. Rather than plan the new room in detail, I simply located the fireplace and doors and got started, giving leeway for spontaneity during the building.

I hired friends to help—one with a genuine feeling for adobe, and another for wood. We rented a small skip-loader and scooped a shallow hole in no time at all. That gave us dirt for all the bricks. As the walls went up we left spaces for windows and turned these into bed-sized window boxes. When we reached ceiling height it became obvious that the trunklike chimney inspired radiating vigas, like the branches of an umbrella tree.

Eight or ten of us, plus three small children, put our muscle and our imagination into the building. The friendships developed became even more important than the construction. One of these new friends was Alan Macrae, who became a partner in this book.

Working with space and adobe is a very familiar experience for anyone who has ever been a potter. A pot, however, once fired becomes hard and brittle while adobe stays malleable. Changes in my life brought changes to my house. We change together.

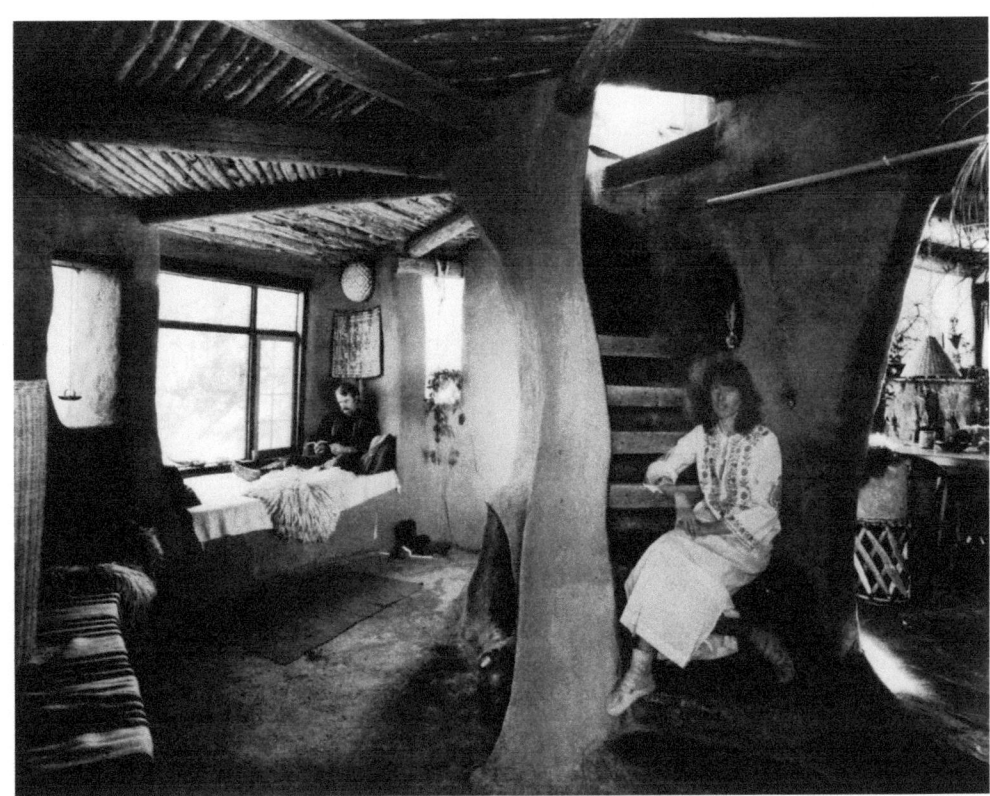

THE WOOLIVERS *had some country land. In 1973, the house they were building burned down. It took a trip to California to help them decide what to do.*

LYNETTE: We knew we had to build something for we'd sold our previous house. On the way back to New Mexico we stopped at coffee shops, and each time we sketched another plan on a paper napkin. We argued it and developed it and by the time we got home we knew what we wanted. We had figured our basic needs and our artistic priorities and worked them together.

It's one thing to have a house and add to it, and quite another to start from scratch; that was scary at first. But I tried to imagine the environment instead of thinking spatially or structurally.

The Woolivers needed a place to live so they bought a lot in town and immediately started construction. The time from ground breaking to moving in was three months.

LYNETTE: We were living in a motel and under pressure to finish the house fast. Every night I had to think about the next day's work. I knew the builders would have questions in the morning and I wanted to be ready with answers. We were both full of ideas, but were limited by the building code, the historical style ordinance, and of course the lack of time. The style ordinance dictated that the southern windows be smaller than we wanted. As it turned out, we would have

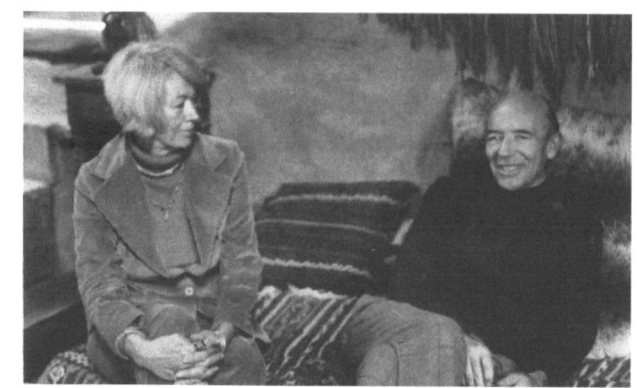

CEREMONIAL SPIRIT

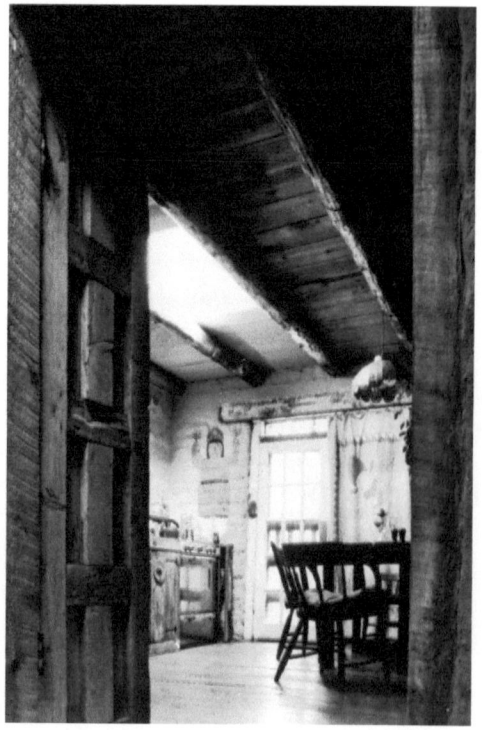

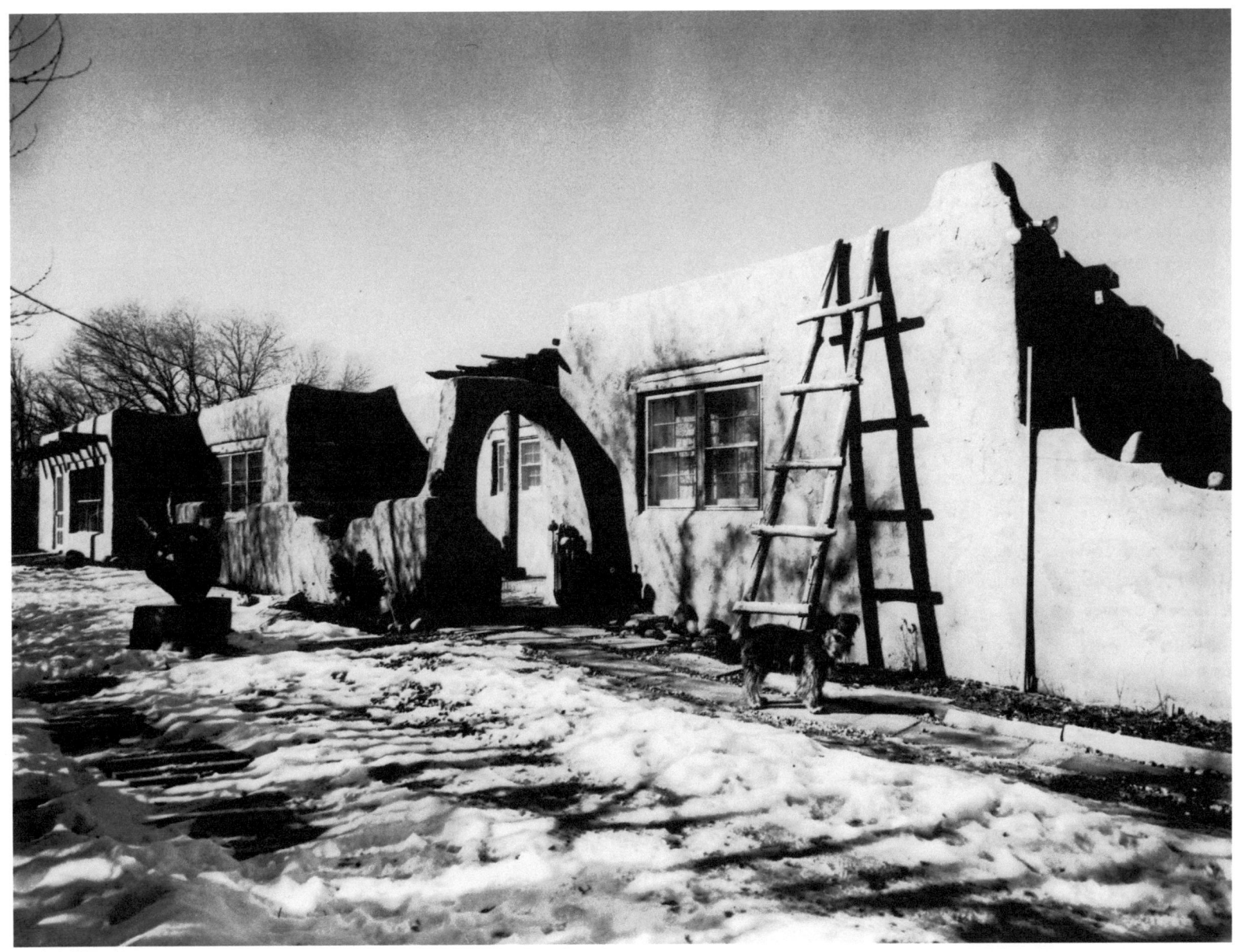

lost the monasterial feeling if we had put in those big windows. So many decisions, such as where to put the skylights, had to be made on the spot.

Lynette teaches t'ai chi ch'uan. She had built a room onto their previous house similar to a Navajo hogan.

LYNETTE: I liked the hogan in every respect except for the big pole in the middle of the room. Every time we had a party people would gather on one side of the pole. That made the oddest psychological division. We arranged this house so the supporting pole is not in the center, yet we kept the hogan feeling by curving the end wall. I like curves—they give a sense of continuity. I also associate a ceremonial feeling with curves, like Indian kivas.

Both George and Lynette are painters. Their studios and bedroom are on one side of the sunken living room, across from the kitchen and dining room. To achieve the effects she wanted, Lynette shaped the fireplace herself, worked on smoothing the adobe walls, arranged the wooden beams for steps, and made the stained glass windows.

LYNETTE: When you work with stone, look at it and visualize something inside, you must hold that concept for a long time, because the hardness and resistance of stone forces you to be determined and keep your original idea firmly in mind. For me there is a relationship between that process and making a house.

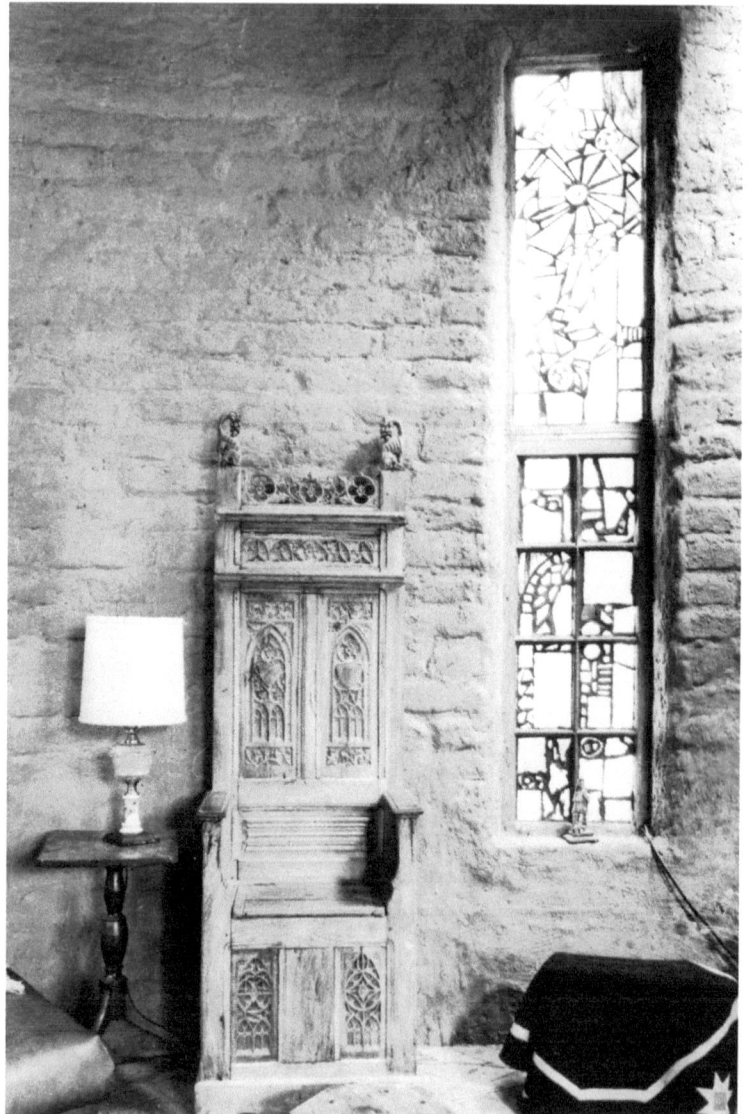

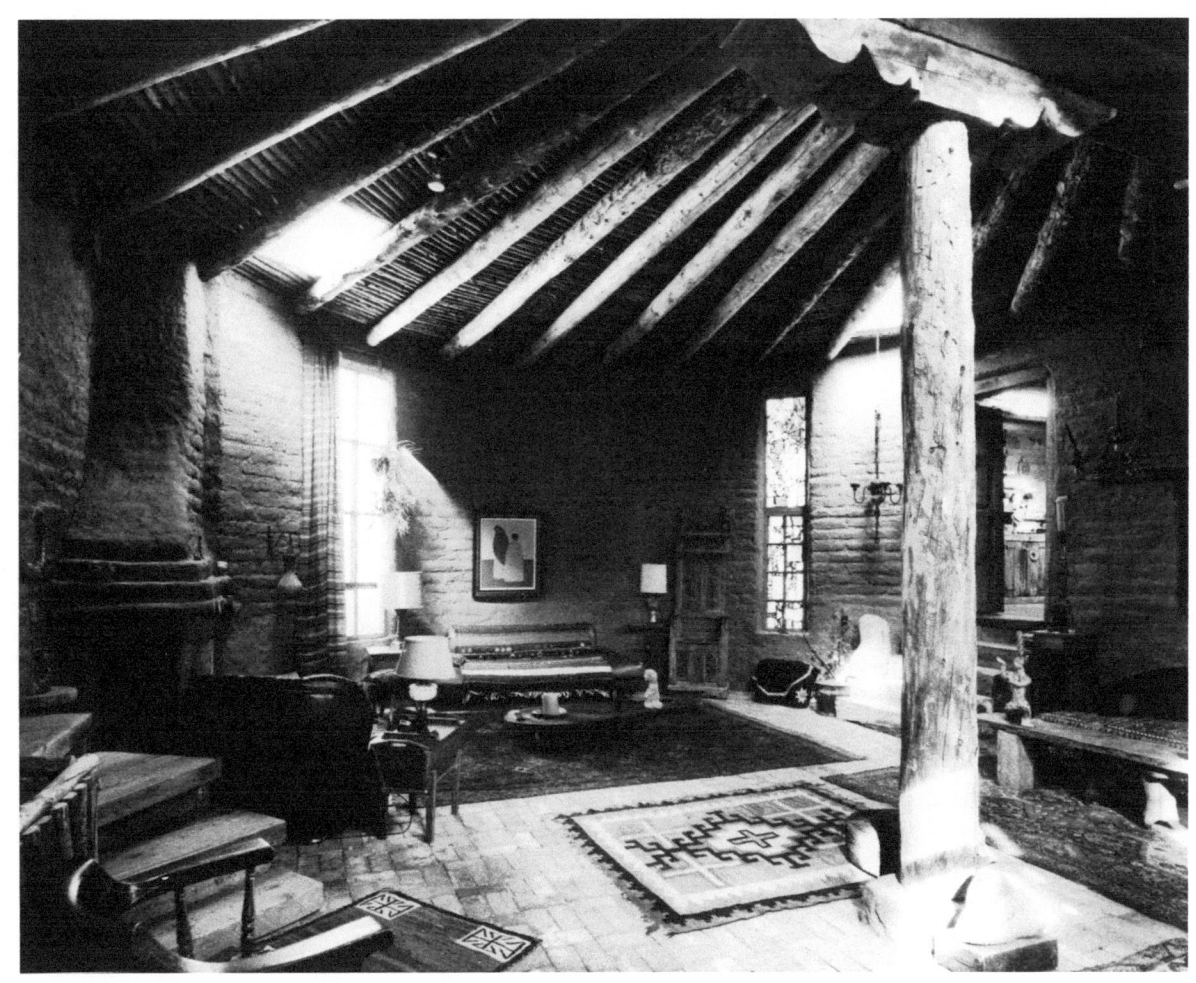

CLIFF DWELLING

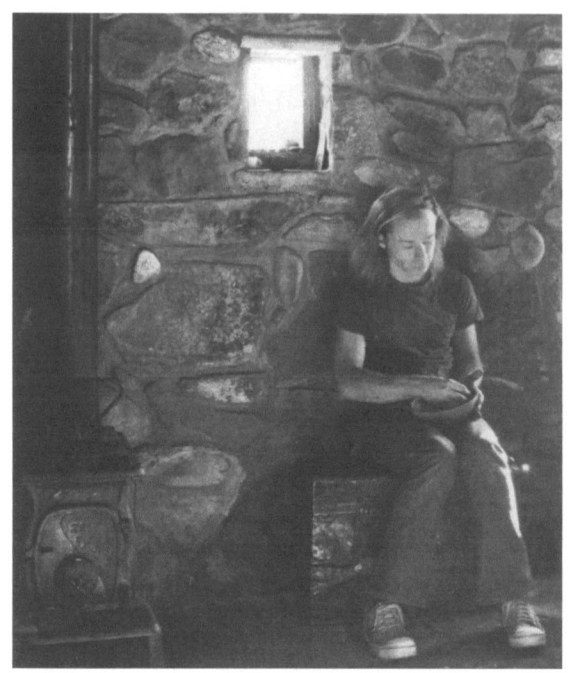

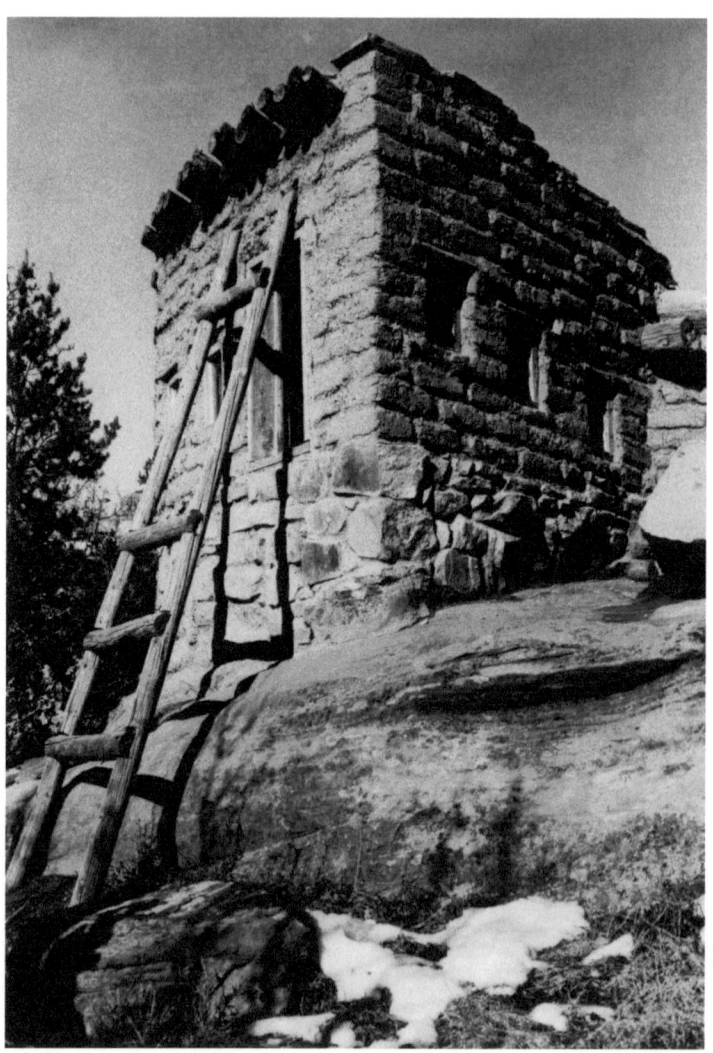

DOUGLAS: I wanted to build a cliff dwelling; looked for a canyon with cliffs, and found this. When I first came, the place was wild. Creatures appeared and checked me out, talked to me. I told them I would live here. We compromised; I stayed, they moved aside.

DOUGLAS JOHNSON *apprenticed to a Spanish stonemason and learned to lay rock.*

I first lived in that little house built onto a cave. I lived there a year and roamed all over the place, watching—the weather, everything.

In Spring 1974 he began his new house.

It took two months to put up the walls in three layers—outer wall, inner wall, and a

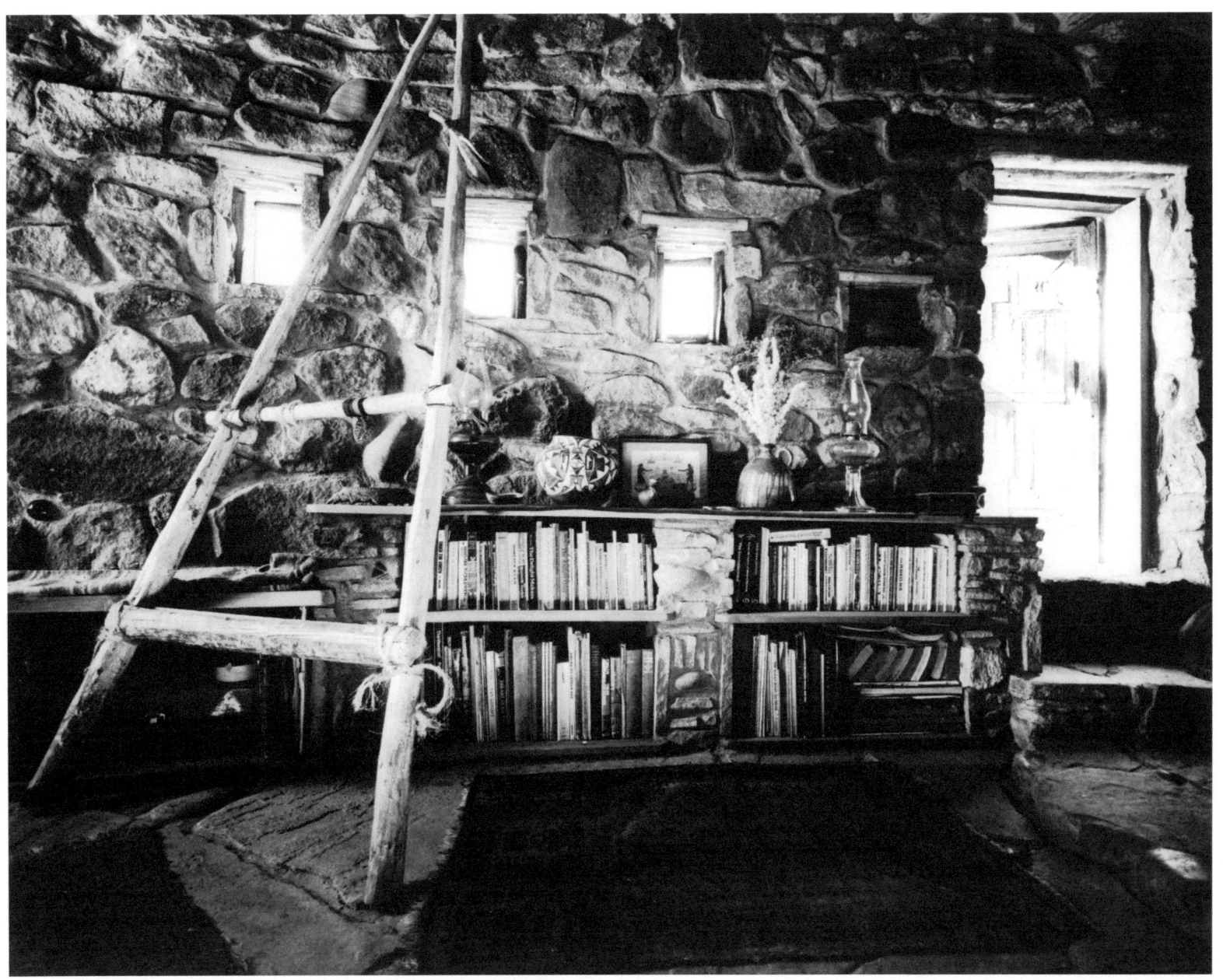

rubble fill. We get four feet of snow and heavy rain up here, so I used cement mortar. It should last five hundred thousand years.

I like the Indian ruins at Chaco Canyon. They used vigas in pairs. It was stylistic—two beams will also support a second-story wall.

The house is Indian style—small windows, small spaces and the way the stones are laid.

On top of the latillas is a mixture of sunflowers, thistles, and wild grasses from a mowed field. That forms a cushion and becomes an insulator. On top of that is tarpaper, then dirt, and finally flagstone. This is the coldest environment, and the warmest house.

Douglas is a successful painter and potter. His work reflects the Indian heritage. He grows crops and trades with local farmers.

That's my easel—painting is the center of my life, the easel is the center of my room. I have more rooms planned. I like to build—building is an art form.

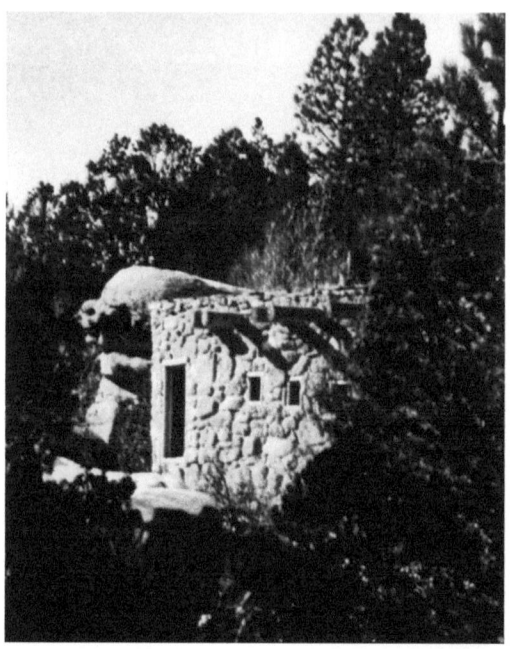

Johnson's second house

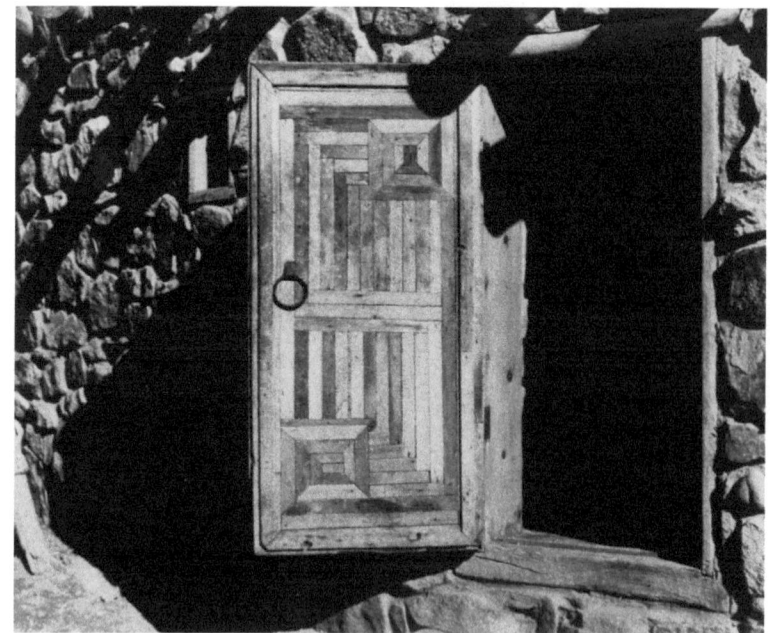

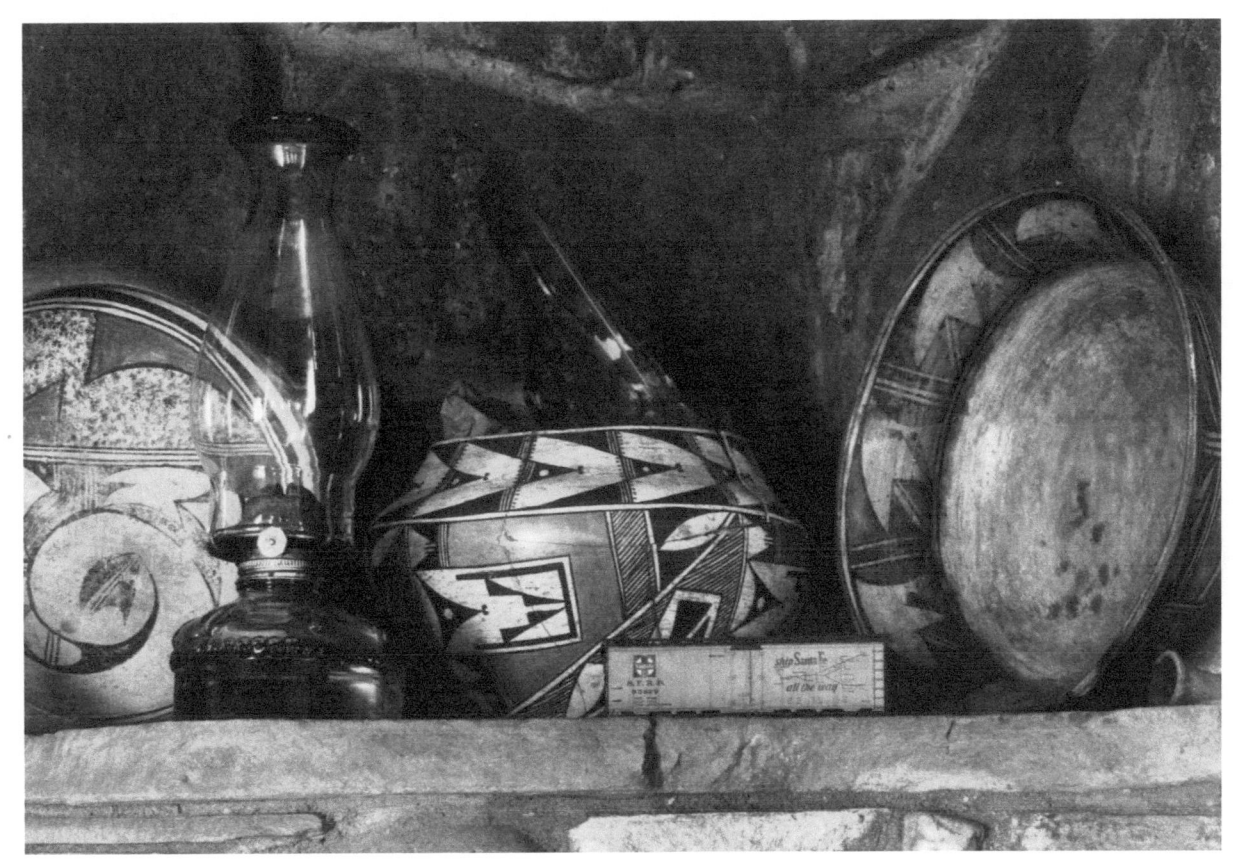

GLOSSARY

ADOBE, a mud of clay, sand and water mixed with straw or manure and either formed into sun-dried bricks or poured to form tapering walls, an Indian method called "puddling." (Adobe: from Spanish *adobar*, to plaster; from Arabic *atob*, sun-dried brick; from Egyptian hieroglyph, d b t.)

CANALES, projecting water spouts to drain the roof.

LATILLAS, aspen poles laid across the vigas to form ceilings.

VIGAS, peeled pine logs hauled from the mountain forests and used as beams.

ZAGUAN, a narrow passageway between two buildings leading to a courtyard.

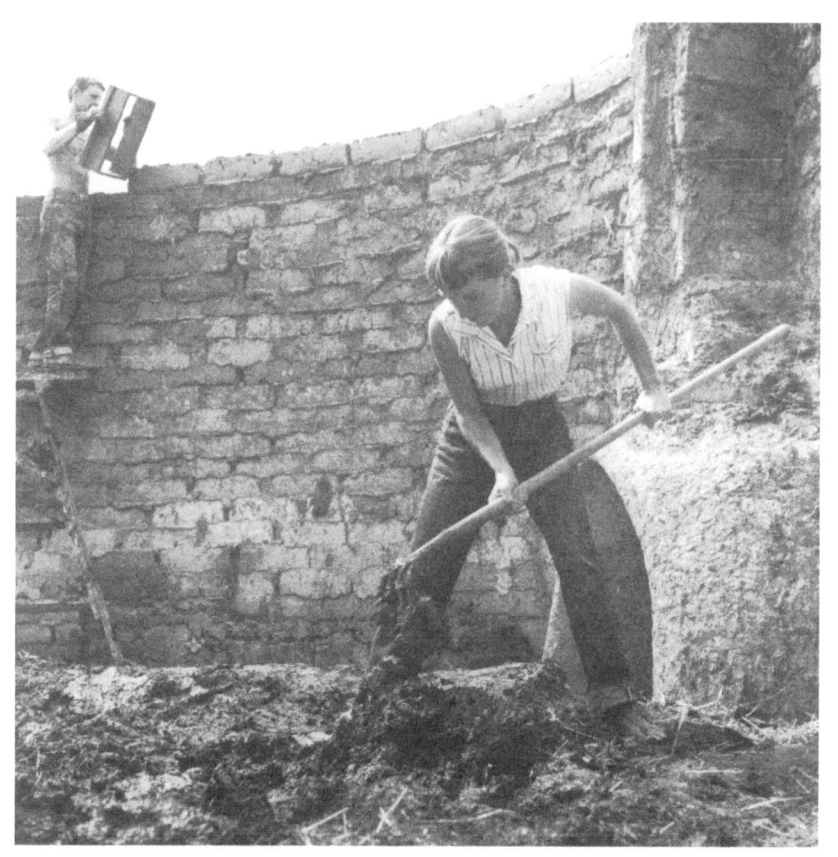

BIBLIOGRAPHY

Adobe Architecture, Myrtle and Wilfred Stedman, Sunstone Press

The Adobe Book, John F. O'Connor, Ancient City Press

Adobe—build it yourself, Paul Graham McHenry, University of Arizona Press

Adobe Construction Methods, University of California Agricultural Experiment Station, Extension Service; L. W. Neubauer

ABC's of Making Adobe Bricks, New Mexico State University Las Cruces: Cooperative Extension Circular 429

Build with Adobe, Marcia Southwick, Sage Books

Adobe and Rammed Earth, United Nations, Housing & Town & Country Planning Bulletin No. 4

Handbook for Building Houses of Earth, Lyle A. Wolfskill, Washington, D.C.: Department of Housing & Urban Development, Division of International Affairs

The Adobe News, published every two months, P.O. Box 702, Los Lunas, New Mexico, 87031

Adobe—Past and Present, William Lumpkins, Museum of New Mexico, Case-Thompson Printing Co.

Making the Adobe Brick, Eugene H. Boudreau, Fifth Street Press

Wayne McCall

PHOTOGRAPHING the "Mud Book" has been an odyssey unparalleled in my experience. From a chance glimpse of the manuscript, to a meeting in a Japanese restaurant in San Francisco, and finally a train trip over the Southwestern desert, I have been involved in a fascinating interlude, between the primal past and a harmonious present.

As I try to relate my experience a montage of images swarms through my head: snow and mud, dark interiors, bright windows and skylights, long exposures, changing bags, cold feet, wide angle perspective, curious children, and camera-shy adults, plus many miles of travel sharing a tiny backseat with Alex, my camera. In these houses prevailed a feeling of mud and childhood fantasies, an adult extension of backyard forts and tree houses. Somehow, to say any more would take away from what my pictures tell about my experience with these people and their houses.

Technical Data: Cameras — Linhof Technika and one old Nikon SP. Lenses — 65 mm Super Angulon and 150 mm Sironar. Film — plus-X 4x5 sheets and plus-X roll film.

Virginia Gray

THE IDEA for this book started some years ago as I looked around at building and realized that the houses I responded to most were built by people for themselves. The individuality and personal warmth stood out.

Building your own house is a great satisfaction for most people. It's a very tangible accomplishment and also means having something to say about how you live—an alternative in a world that is increasingly remote and impersonal. All the people in these pages were open and enthusiastic about their building and sharing their experiences with us.

In the process of making the book there were times I found it difficult to get on with the business of taking pictures and turning on the tape recorder. I wanted to just *be* with the people and their houses; sit against a wall protected from the wind in the warm sun and savor the uniqueness of that particular person and place.

Alan Macrae

WHEN I WAS ASKED about this book I had a hard time answering. It's not only about adobe building, it's about people. A house is an expression of the people who build it and live in it.

New Mexico has an expansive spirit that may never be tamed. This has been imparted to these houses in a special way. Logs, adobe bricks, mud plaster, and stone are mixed with solar heating, sculpture, and greenhouses—the earth and her spirit. The spirit of tradition *and* innovation still exists.

Working on this book I did a lot of driving, walking, knocking on doors, taking photos and asking questions. Strangers introduced me to their friends and neighbors. It was exciting not only discovering and exploring new houses, but meeting these people. They, their approach to living, and the spirit of their houses gives me new energy in my own work as a builder. I did this book because I wanted to share that energy with others.

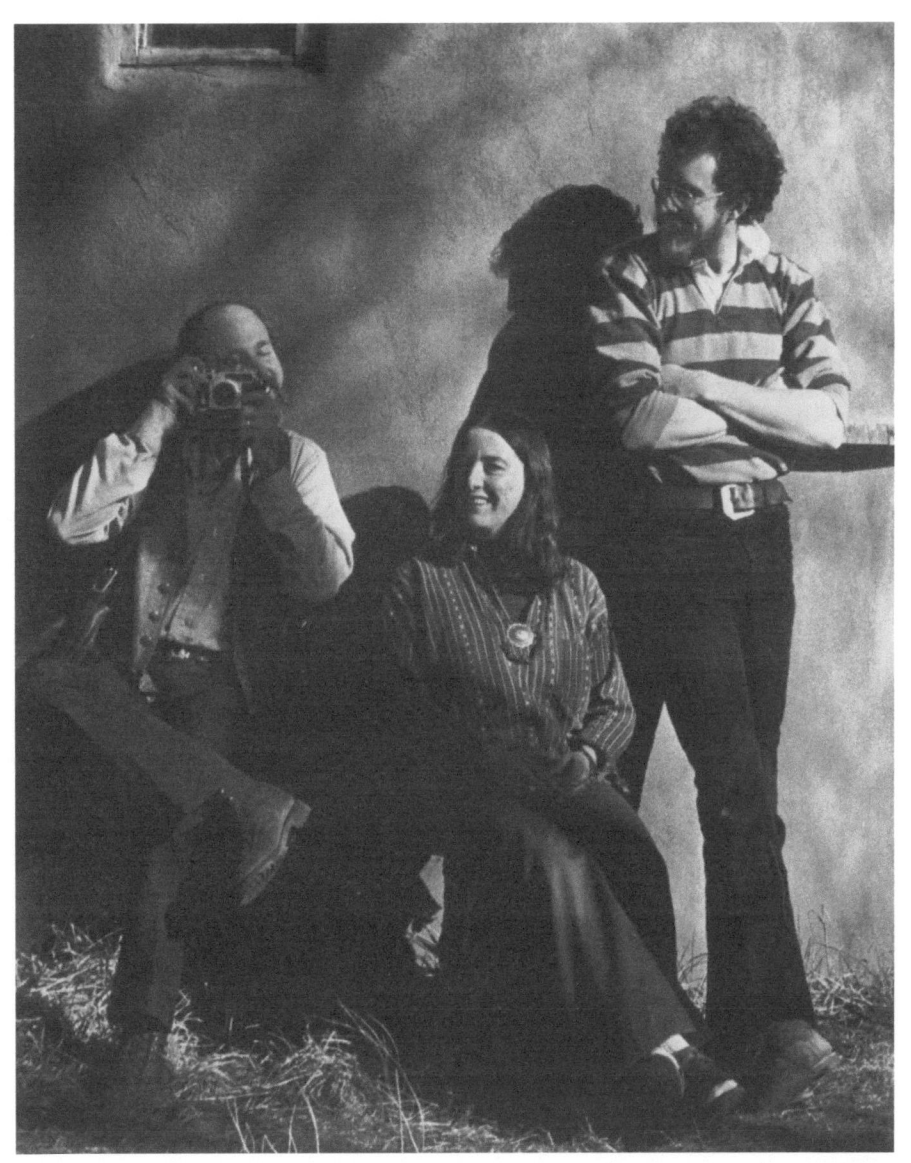

SPECIAL THANKS

To Robert S. Mandel for invaluable suggestions; to Stephanie Sanchez for the *enjarradora* drawing, page 11; to Corinne Machado for drawing of McGowan house, page 10; to Charlie Ramsberg for drawing, pages 14-15; to Alex Cole for photo, page 12; to John Collier, Jr. for photos, pages 44 (left), 90; to Dan Winston, Karl Kernberger, Peter Hayes, Paul Willis, and to all those who enthusiastically added life to these pages by allowing themselves to be photographed, especially Laurie Macrae, Dan Bush, Leon Elder, Georgie McGowan and Kathy Mandel; and to Megan Macrae for her continual support.

Our special appreciation for all the people, in this book and not, who shared their houses and parts of their lives with us.

PRODUCTION

Composition by Mackintosh & Young; display type by Bill Horton; editorial and design assistance by Linda Rolens; and graphic assistance by Alice Barnwell and Jerry Wright.

Photos by Alan Macrae: pages 20 l., 42 upper l., upper r., lower r., 43 lower l., lower r., 46 lower, 50 upper l., lower, 52 upper l., 58, 62 upper l., 64 l., 68, 72 l., 80 upper. Photos by Virginia Gray: pages 20 r., 36 l., 37, 72 r., 86. Photo by Noel Young: page 93.

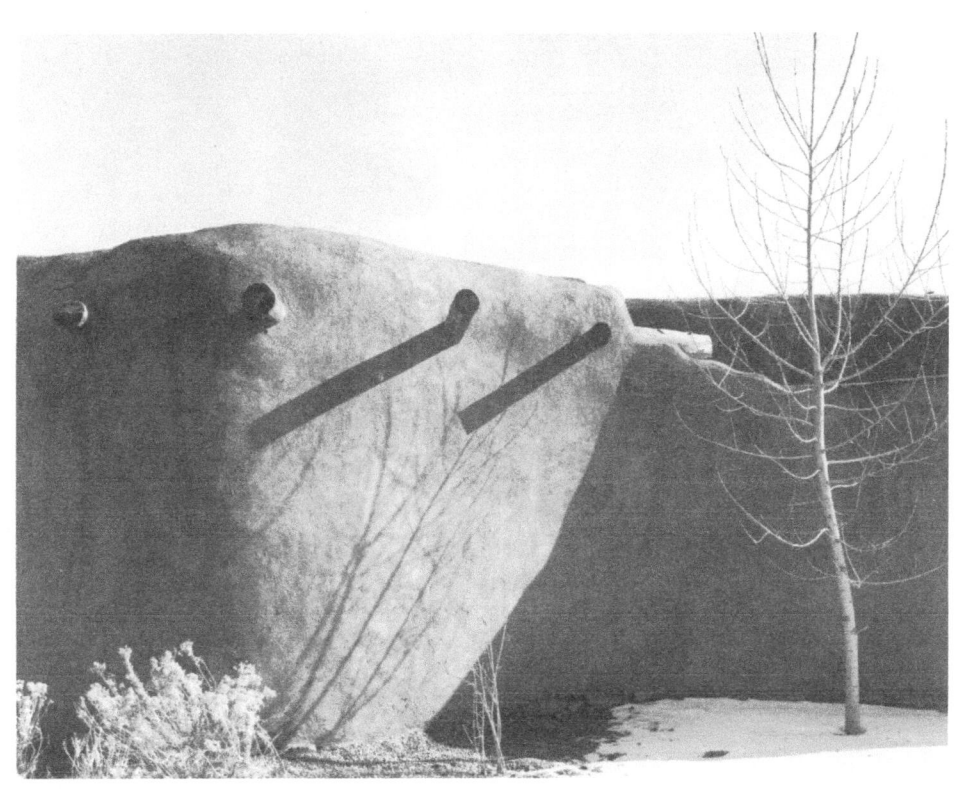

www.ingramcontent.com/pod-product-compliance
Lightning Source LLC
Chambersburg PA
CBHW042320210526

45473CB00008B/2402